C I T Y P A C K

Toronto

*Laurie McIntosh
8630 Redwood Dr
Vienna VA 22180*

By Marilyn Wood

L2laurie@aol.com

Fodor's
2ND EDITION

Fodor's Travel Publications, Inc.
New York • Toronto • London • Sydney • Auckland

WWW.FODORS.COM

Contents

About this book

KEY TO SYMBOLS

✚ map reference on the fold-out map accompanying this book (see below)

✉ address

☎ telephone number

🕐 opening times

🍴 restaurant or café on premises or nearby

🚇 nearest subway train station

🚉 nearest overground train station

🚌 nearest tram and bus routes

⛴ nearest riverboat or ferry stop

♿ facilities for visitors with disabilities

✋ admission charge

↔ other nearby places of interest

❓ tours, lectures, or special events

➤ indicates the page where you will find a fuller description

ℹ tourist information

Citypack Toronto is divided into six sections to cover the six most important aspects of your visit to Toronto. It includes:

- An introduction to the city and its people
- Itineraries, walks, and excursions
- The top 25 sights to visit—as selected by the author
- Features about different aspects of the city that make it special
- Detailed listings of restaurants, hotels, stores, and nightlife
- Practical information

In addition, easy-to-read side panels provide fascinating extra facts and snippets, highlights of places to visit and invaluable practical advice.

CROSS-REFERENCES

To help you make the most of your visit, cross-references, indicated by ➤, show you where to find additional information about a place or subject.

MAPS

The fold-out map in the wallet at the back of the book is a comprehensive street plan of Toronto. All the map references given in the book refer to this map. For example, the CN Tower on Front Street West has the following information: ✚ J9—indicating the grid square of the map in which the CN Tower will be found.

The downtown map found on the inside front and back covers of the book itself are for quick reference. They show the top 25 sights in the city, described on pages 24–48, which are clearly plotted by number (**1**–**25**, not page number) from west to east.

TORONTO *life*

5

INTRODUCING TORONTO

Cultural Toronto

No one figure or group of figures can summarize the city's cultural attributes. In music Toronto gave us classical musician Glenn Gould, up-and-coming The Barenaked Ladies, and contemporary country Blue Rodeo. It is often the backdrop to the novels of Margaret Atwood and Robertson Davies, and to the films of Atom Egoyan and David Cronenberg. The actor William Shatner, famous for his *Star Trek* role, is from Toronto, as is *Scream* actress Neve Campbell. Mass communicators will always associate the city with Marshall McLuhan whose catchphrase was "the media is the message," while to theatergoers it is the birthplace of such greats as Mary Pickford and Raymond Massey.

Tell people you are going to Toronto and they will probably ask what on earth for. Whatever possible reason could you have to visit Toronto the Good, where the sidewalks are almost free of people at 8PM and the shops are shuttered on Sundays? Well, maybe they would have had reason to scoff 25 years ago, but today the city has risen to become one of the world's leaders: in 1996 it was chosen by *Fortune* as the number one city outside the United States for work and family life, ahead of London, Paris, and Singapore.

This new Toronto is a vibrant, cosmopolitan city bursting with entrepreneurial energy and ethnic diversity. As you come in from the airport one of the first things that will strike you is the needle of the CN Tower piercing the sky, and the cluster of buildings around it that make up the downtown skyline. On a sunny day, other strong images will be the blue waters of the lake and the parklands that run alongside it, two immediately visible physical features of the city. Once downtown, you will discover a mixture of historic and contemporary architecture—solid

Toronto's skyline, dominated by its famous CN Tower

Romanesque-revival masterpieces contrasting with skyscrapers and handsome Victorian residences. The flavors of the different neighborhoods will quickly assert themselves and leave their impression, from hip Queen Street West to upscale Yorkville, from Chinatown to Little Italy, from the Caribbean-Portuguese Kensington Market to Greektown, and from the quirky beaches on the lake to moneyed Rosedale.

No longer a bastion of Anglophile conservatism, the city has blossomed, with restaurants and cafés offering all kinds of ethnic cuisines and an annual calendar that is punctuated by all manner of multicultural festivals. Both developments reflect the increasing diversity of the city's population, which now represents more than 80 different ethnic groups speaking more than 100 languages. Toronto now has Canada's largest immigrant community. The first major wave of immigration occurred at the turn of the century when Chinese, Greeks, Italians, Jews, Ukrainians and Poles came to build the railroads, work Ontario's mines and man the growing industries. The second wave took place after World War II,

Curtain up

Ed and David Mirvish, Toronto's father and son theatrical producers, are mounting the Canadian premiere of Disney's award-winning *The Lion King* at their beautiful Princess of Wales Theatre in Toronto. *The Lion King* is the biggest success in Broadway history, with tickets selling out up to two years in advance. The Toronto production opens in April 2000 and has become the most sought-after ticket in Canada.

Honest Ed

Ed Mirvish is one of Toronto's great impresarios and a living legend. It was the discount store Honest Ed's that brought him fame and fortune. Always a theater lover, in 1963 he bought the Royal Alexandra for the bargain price of $200,000 and converted surrounding warehouses into restaurants. In 1982, when the owners of London's Old Vic were seeking buyers to save the theater, Ed audaciously outbid Andrew Lloyd Webber. He was later awarded the prestigious CBE honor by the Queen for his efforts. With his son David, he built the Princess of Wales Theatre, opened in 1993.

View of Toronto from the CN Tower

and in the 1960s, '70s and '80s, when immigrants arrived from Asia, Africa, and the Caribbean— Vietnamese, Koreans, Cambodians, Indians and Pakistanis, Ghanaians, Kenyans, Ethiopians, and Somalis, Trinidadians, Jamaicans, Barbadians, Haitians, Guyanese, and many more. Each group has enriched the city with its cuisine, music, dance, religion, language, and rhythm of life.

Today the civility and attributes that have made Toronto so attractive are in danger of destruction, according to some resident commentators, such as author and urban planner Jane Jacobs. They object to the sweeping changes that have been pushed through by the Progressive Conservative Provincial Government to amalgamate six municipalities to create one "megacity" presided over by North York mayor, Mel Lastman. The new government debuted in January 1998, but the full effect on the community has yet to be seen. The mayor's office says "We eliminated 60 percent of our senior management staff and saved $17 million a year. We are now dealing with one financial institution instead of seven for more yearly savings. We took the old departments from the old governments and merged them into new cost-effective divisions. In total, we have saved taxpayers $120 million a year."

Meanwhile, despite rapid growth and change, the city has managed to preserve a gentle demeanor and feel for tradition. And while the diversity of the population sometimes results in racial tension, the city retains a strong sense of community which is clearly exhibited in the clean, safe streets and public facilities. The attitudes that informed the Loyalist founders of Canada—peace, order, and good government—still resonate in Toronto and the city represents a pleasant compromise between the unbridled freedom of the U.S. and the conservatism and social hierarchy of many European countries.

TORONTO IN FIGURES

People
- City population: 750,000
- Metro population (includes the cities of Toronto, North York, Etobicoke, Scarborough and York): 3.5 million
- Greater Toronto (includes the City and Metro areas): 4.26 million
- Non-Canadians: 41 percent
- 62 percent of city dwellers are under 44
- 42 percent of city dwellers are single
- 1.4 million vehicles enter Metro daily
- 7 percent of residents commute by bicycle
- 13 percent of Torontonians attend church regularly
- 44 percent of residents own pets

Geography
- Metro Toronto Area: 392 square miles
- Streets: 530 miles
- Bicycle pathways: 50 miles
- Subway track: 36.3 miles
- TTC (Toronto Transit Commission) operates 1,943 miles of routes
- Average number of days per year below 32°F: 147
- Average number of days per year 32°F or above: 4
- Latitude: 43° north, roughly the same as northern Spain or northern California
- Distance from New York: 495 miles

Leisure & Tourism
- Visitors: 20.2 million (1997)
- Hotel rooms: 32,030 (1995)
- Restaurants: more than 4,000
- Ethnic restaurants: about 2,000
- Theater venues: 70
- 10 miles of waterfront and 9,778 acres of parkland

A CHRONOLOGY

1720 France sets up trading post at Toronto.

1751 Fort Rouille built.

1763 Treaty of Paris secures Canada for England.

1787 The British purchase land from the Mississauga tribe on which Toronto will be sited.

1793 John Graves Simcoe, Governor of Upper Canada, arrives and names settlement York.

1813 Americans invade, destroy Fort York, and burn Parliament Buildings.

1834 City named Toronto (meaning "meeting-place"). William Lyon Mackenzie becomes first mayor.

1837 Rebellion against the Family Compact (the group controlling government), led by former mayor Mackenzie (➤ 12), sparked by recession.

1844 First City Hall built; George Brown founds *The Globe*.

1845 University opens with establishment of King's College.

1851 St. Lawrence Hall built.

1852 Toronto Stock Exchange opens.

1858 Toronto Islands created from a peninsula smashed by violent storm.

1867 Canadian Confederation: Toronto becomes capital of Ontario province.

1869 Eaton's department store opens (➤ 70).

1884 Streets lit by electricity.

1886 Provincial Parliament buildings erected.

1896 National Canadian magazine, *MacLean's Magazine*, started.

1906	Toronto Symphony founded.
1907	Royal Alexandra Theatre opens.
1912	Royal Ontario Museum founded.
1914–18	70,000 Torontonians enlist, 13,000 killed in World War I.
1920	Group of Seven's first art exhibition (➤ 12).
1923	Chinese Exclusion Act restricted Chinese immigration.
1930s	Depression: 30 percent unemployment in 1933.
1931	Maple Leaf Gardens ice-hockey arena built.
1950	Sunday sports permitted.
1953	Metro (metropolitan Toronto) organized.
1965	New City Hall built.
1971	Ontario Place—waterfront entertainment area—built.
1972	Harbourfront under development.
1975	CN Tower opens.
1989	SkyDome stadium opens.
1992	Blue Jays win World Series (and in 1993).
1993	CBC Building open.
1995	Progressive Conservative Government elected. Focus on budget cuts.
1996	*Fortune* names Toronto "Best City for Work and Family outside the U.S."
1998	Megacity debuts.
1999	Last game played at Maple Leaf Gardens.

People & Events from History

Historic street names

Many prominent families are recalled in Toronto's street names. Two examples are Jarvis Street, named for William Jarvis, a New England loyalist who became Provincial Secretary, and Beverley, which refers to Virginia loyalist John Beverley who, age 22, became Attorney General, and was later Chief Justice of Upper Canada, the region's administrative home until the province was formally named.

WILLIAM LYON MACKENZIE & THE REBELLION OF 1837

The first mayor of Toronto, Willilam Lyon Mackenzie, shared immigrant aspirations for political reform and campaigned vehemently against the narrow-minded, exclusive power of the Family Compact—a small group of WASPs who controlled the city's economy and politics. By 1837 he was advocating open rebellion, and on December 5, a group of around 700 rebels assembled at Montgomery's Tavern. Led by Mackenzie, they marched on the city. The sheriff called out the militia, who scattered the rebels at Carlton Street. Mackenzie fled to the United States. Two other ringleaders were hanged.

THE GROUP OF SEVEN

As the city became larger and wealthier in the early 20th century it attracted artists. Among them were J. H. MacDonald, Arthur Lismer, Frank Johnston, Franklin Carmichael, Lawren Harris, Frederick Varley, and A. Y. Jackson, who became known as the Group of Seven when their works were shown in a joint salon in 1920. They shared a desire to paint the unique Canadian landscape and sought to reflect the nation's identity. Their subject became the forests, rivers, and mountains of the country's wilderness.

*Lawren Harris,
Decorative Landscape,
detail*

ISLAND SURVIVORS

Some 600 or so artists, schoolteachers, and aging activists live on idyllic Algonquin and Ward's Islands, occupying modest cottages and getting by with few amenities and no cars. Their survival is the outcome of a dramatic struggle. In 1956 the local government decided to evict the residents and to convert the islands into public parkland. Bulldozers moved in and 600 buildings were flattened, but when attempts were made to remove the last enclave, the residents formed a phalanx against the onslaught, placing their children in front. A bitter court fight ended in 1992 when the islanders were granted the right to purchase 99-year leases to their properties.

TORONTO
how to organize your time

13

ITINERARIES

In a two- or three-day visit it is impossible to see all of Toronto because at least seven of the top attractions lie outside the downtown core. Choose your personal favorites and focus on them—what follows are merely guidelines to help you devise your own personalized tours.

ITINERARY ONE	**DOWNTOWN WEST**
Morning	Start early by catching the trolley out to historic Fort York (➤ 29), where in summer you can see soldiers drilling and firing cannon. Walk from here to catch the tour of the SkyDome (➤ 35). The CN Tower (➤ 36) is next door—ride up for the panoramic vista.
Lunch	At one of the many restaurants in King Street West near John Street or on Front Street.
Afternoon	Have a look at the impressive Old City Hall, then visit the Art Gallery of Ontario (➤ 37) and the Grange (➤ 38) by way of the new City Hall fronted by Nathan Phillips Square (➤ 43), where you might feel like taking a break.
Sunset	West along Dundas is the heart of Chinatown. Dine here or, if it's a livelier scene you have in mind, move south to hip Queen Street with its bistros and clubs.
ITINERARY TWO	**THE DON VALLEY**
Morning	Spend the morning at Ontario Science Centre (➤ 47). Get there as soon as it opens to enjoy the hundreds of interactive exhibits as freely as possible.
Lunch	At the Science Centre or at the next stop, Toronto Zoo (➤ 48).
Afternoon	Follow the zoo's marked pathways to the Continental pavilions.
Sunset	Head out to the Danforth, or Greektown, for dinner and an evening with a distinctly Greek flavor.

ITINERARY THREE	**MIDTOWN**
Morning	Stroll through the grounds of the University of Toronto (➤ 33) viewing the varied architecture. Visit the offbeat and engaging Bata Shoe Museum (➤ 32) and then head three blocks east to see the Royal Ontario Museum's diverse collections (➤ 39) or the inspiring collection of china and ceramics in the George R. Gardiner Museum of Ceramic Art (➤ 40) across the road.
Lunch	At the ROM (Jamie Kennedy, one of Toronto's top chefs, presides here—or, if you are on a budget, there's a cafeteria). Otherwise take your pick of Yorkville's many bistros, cafés, and restaurants.
Afternoon	Head over to Yorkville, the city's premier shopping and gallery district. Don't miss Hazelton Lanes. Walk or ride to Casa Loma (➤ 30), castle-residence of early entrepreneur industrialist Sir Henry Pellatt.
Sunset	Linger at one of Yorkville's many outdoor café-bars (weather permitting) before choosing a restaurant for dinner.
ITINERARY FOUR	**THE NORTHERN FRINGE**
Morning	You really need a car to follow this itinerary. Start early for Black Creek Pioneer Village (➤ 27), where you can step back into the 19th century. Nearby are the thrills of Canada's Wonderland theme park (➤ 26, you could spend all day here).
Lunch	At Canada's Wonderland or at the Doctor's House in Kleinburg.
Afternoon	Visit the McMichael Collection of Canadian art (➤ 25), before going downtown via the highways.
Sunset	Back in town, enjoy a leisurely walk along Harbourfront (➤ 42) or, in summer, visit Ontario Place theme park (➤ 28).

WALKS

The Gooderham building

DOWNTOWN HIGHLIGHTS

Walk east from the CN Tower along Front Street to check out the lobby-studios and museum of the CBC Building. Backtrack along Front and turn right up John Street to King Street. Drop into the Metro Hall for general information and to see the public art, then cross King Street to see the Frank Stella murals in the Princess of Wales Theatre. Cruise east past Ed Mirvish's extraordinary restaurants (some have closed down) along with his Royal Alexandra Theatre (➤ 8). On the south side of King at Simcoe Street don't miss the flying-saucer-like Roy Thomson Hall. Continue on King to York Street and the Exchange Tower (Canadian Sculpture Society's gallery and Toronto Stock Exchange); at King and Bay Streets rises Mies van der Rohe's Toronto Dominion Centre. For a sharp architectural contrast drop into the grand banking hall of the Canadian Imperial Bank of Commerce on King and Yonge. Backtrack to Bay and turn south to Royal Bank Plaza and, across from it, the entrance to the BCE Building (Hockey Hall of Fame). Continue east along Front to the St. Lawrence Centre for the Arts and the historic storefronts on the south side of the street. Note the unusual "Flatiron" or Gooderham building in the center of Front. Cross Church Street and keep walking to the St. Lawrence Market (➤ 46). Backtrack to Church and turn north to King and St. James' Cathedral (➤ 54). From the Cathedral walk west on King to Bay. Turn north for Old City Hall, then west on Queen with the expanse of the public square in front of New City Hall. Queen leads west past Osgoode Hall and Campbell House to the retro stores lining the street farther on.

THE SIGHTS

- CN Tower (➤ 36)
- CBC Building (➤ 60)
- Metro Hall (➤ 59)
- Princess of Wales Theatre (➤ 59)
- Queen Street (➤ 51, 70)

INFORMATION

Distance 1.2 miles
Time 1½ hours
Start point CN Tower
✚ J9
🚇 Union
End point Queen Street West at Spadina
✚ H8
🚊 Queen Street West streetcar

16

MIDTOWN HITS

Turn your back on the front facade of the Ontario Provincial Parliament Buildings, walk south to College Street and turn right. At King's College Road take another right and walk through the front campus of the University of Toronto. Take King's College Circle west to Tower Road. En route, on your left will be University College opposite the Stewart Observatory. Carry on north to Hart House (➤ 33, 54) and Soldier's Memorial Tower. Turn right along Hoskin Avenue to Trinity College and then proceed east toward Queen's Park. Go left on Avenue Road, walking north past the Royal Ontario Museum and the George R. Gardiner Museum. Turn right on fashionable Bloor Street (which could be described as the Fifth Avenue of Toronto), then left on Yonge Street to Cumberland Street and walk west. You are now in the heart of Yorkville, Toronto's fashionable shopping mecca. Turn down Old York Lane to Yorkville Avenue. Cross Yorkville and go down Hazelton Lane to the Hazelton Lanes Complex where all the contemporary designer stores can be found. Come back out the way you went in and browse through the galleries on Hazelton Avenue. Backtrack to Yorkville Avenue and go left along it to Bay Street; cross Bay. Note the old Firehall and then the Yorkville Public Library, both on the left. Continue to Yonge. Turn right and cross the street to the light and airy Metro Library and walk south to the Bloor-Yonge subway stop.

THE SIGHTS

- Ontario Parliament Buildings (➤ 41)
- University College (➤ 33)
- Stewart Observatory
- Hart House (➤ 33)
- Soldier's Memorial Tower
- Royal Ontario Museum (➤ 39)
- George R. Gardiner Museum (➤ 40)
- Bloor Street
- Yorkville (➤ 51, 70)
- Hazelton Lanes (➤ 70)
- Firehall
- Metro Library (➤ 52)
- Yorkville Public Library

INFORMATION

Distance 1.8 miles
Time 2 hours
Start point Ontario Parliament Buildings
🚇 J7
🚊 Queen's Park
End point Bloor/Yonge Streets
🚇 K6
🚊 Bloor-Yonge

Toronto's downtown skyline

17

EVENING STROLLS

Night falls on the city

QUEEN STREET WEST

Any time of day, Queen Street West is full of life, but the tempo picks up in the evenings when the pierced-nose-and-lip crowd gathers at spots like Rivoli and Bamboo. Start your walk just west of Simcoe Street and stroll along either side of the street. There's plenty of intriguing window-shopping to do and some stores stay open late. You will find contemporary and secondhand bookstores, retro and up-to-the-minute fashion stores, craft galleries, and junk stores such as the Queen's Trade Centre at No. 635. At the corner of John Street, check out Citytv's Speaker's Corner, where you can record any gripes you have about the city. Along the way, among the favorite restaurants, bars, and cafés are Le Select, the Rivoli, and the Gypsy Co-op which, at No. 815, is as far as you will probably want to explore safely.

LITTLE ITALY

In summer one of the best places to take a *passeggiata* is in Little Italy along College Street between Euclid and Shaw Streets (► 51). Here, in the early and late evening crowds gather at the cafés, bars, and restaurants. The possibilities are endless. Go into Bar Italia for a game of pool in the comfortable upstairs pool parlor, or El Convento Rico, a Latin hot-spot with gay and hetero bars. Stop at the old-fashioned Café Diplomatico, taste superb ice cream at Sicilian Ice Cream or hang out at one of the more trendy spots like Souz Dal (► 83).

THE DANFORTH (GREEKTOWN)

This Greek community on the east side of the city has a lively night scene. Along here you will find cafés and bakeries, Greek specialty stores—and taverna after taverna (► 51).

INFORMATION

Distance 1.7 miles
Time 1¼ hours
Start point Queen Street West at Simcoe
➕ J8
🚇 Osgoode
End point Queen Street West at Niagara Street
➕ G8
🚋 Queen Street West streetcar

INFORMATION

Distance 0.6 miles
Time 30 minutes–1 hour
Start point College Street at Euclid
➕ G7
🚋 College Street streetcar
End point College Street at Shaw
➕ F7
🚋 College Street streetcar

INFORMATION

Distance 0.5 miles
Time 30 minutes
Start point Bowden Street
➕ M6
🚇 Chester
End point Pape Avenue
➕ N6
🚇 Pape

ORGANIZED SIGHTSEEING

A CHOICE OF TOURS

The easy way to orient yourself is to board one of the double-decker buses operated by Olde Town Toronto Tours Ltd ☎ 416/368-6877 or, in summer only, a regular bus operated by Grayline Tours ☎ 416/594-3310. For a more exciting view, try a seven-minute helicopter tour given by National Helicopters ☎ 905/893-2727 from the island airport.

WALKING TOURS

Some of the best tours are led by Shirley Lum of Taste of the World ☎ 416/923-6813. Shirley includes stops in stores, temples, small factories, and restaurants. She covers several neighborhoods— Chinatown, the Kensington and St. Lawrence Markets, Yorkville and Rosedale—and also operates bike tours. Heritage Toronto offers summer walking tours ☎ 416/463-9233 or 392-6827.

Hazelton Avenue, Yorkville

HARBOUR TOURS

The best way to see the skyline is from a boat in the harbor. The most impressive vessel— the three-masted schooner *The Challenge* operated by Great Lakes Schooner Company ☎ 416/260-6355—offers one- and two-hour cruises. Amsterdam-style glass-enclosed boats operated by Toronto Tours ☎ 416/869-1372 also cruise the harbor and islands, leaving from Queen's Quay West.

CULTURAL TOURS

Backstage tours of the Elgin and Wintergarden theaters are available. If you would like insight into the workings of the Canadian Broadcasting Company (CBC) and want to tour the sets of some favorite comedy shows, then take the tour at the CBC; CHUM/Citytv tours (CHUM is a radio station) give you a hipper, very different media experience.

View of the CN Tower from the harbor

19

EXCURSIONS

INFORMATION

Stratford
Distance 93 miles
Time 1½ hours
🚌 Public Transit Greyhound
☎ 416/367-8747 or
1/800-661-8747 to
Kitchener then Cha-Co
Trails ☎ 519/681-2861
to Stratford
🚆 VIA Rail ☎ 416/366-
8411 or 1/800-561-8630
to Stratford
➕ Off map to west
ℹ Information Centre Tourism
Stratford
✉ 88 Wellington Street,
ON N5A 6W1
☎ 519/271-5140

Niagara Falls
Distance 80 miles
Time 1½ hours
🚌 Public Transit Greyhound
☎ 416/367-8747 or
1/800-661-8747
➕ Off map to south
ℹ Niagara Falls Canada
Visitor and Convention
Bureau
✉ 5515 Stanley Avenue,
ON L2G 3X4
☎ 905/356-6061
The Niagara Parks
Commission
✉ Box 150, 7400 Portage
Road South, ON L2E 6T2
☎ 905/356-2241

STRATFORD

Stratford is an attractive Victorian town with good shops for browsing, a riverfront park, and several very fine restaurants. There are swans on the Avon River and Shakespeare productions on the boards in the three theaters at the Stratford Theatre Festival. Beginning modestly in 1953, when Sir Alec Guinness played Richard III on a stage in a huge tent, the festival now has many famous alumni, among them Dame Maggie Smith, Sir Peter Ustinov, Alan Bates, Christopher Plummer, Julie Harris, and William Hurt. Performances begin mid-May and run through mid-November. In addition to the productions, visitors can enjoy discussions with actors and directors, and take backstage and warehouse tours. Nearby, visit Shakespeare for its antiques shops, St. Mary's for its Victorian architecture, and Kitchener-Waterloo, home of an *Oktoberfest* and of a thriving Saturday Mennonite market.

NIAGARA FALLS

This natural wonder of the world is on most visitors' itineraries. The Canadian side of the falls is far superior to the American; the 35-mile-long Niagara Parkway winds along the Niagara River from Chippawa to Niagara-on-the-Lake past orchards, wineries, parks, and shady picnic areas—a joy for biking and hiking. The area immediately around the falls, especially near Clifton Hill, is spotted with many shoddy commercial outlets but the falls are nonetheless magnificent at any time of the year, even in winter. Unmissable sights at the falls include a ride aboard the *Maid of the Mist* and the Spanish Aero Car, the botanical gardens of the School of Horticulture, the Niagara Parks Butterfly

A world-famous sight—Niagara Falls

The splendor of the Niagara Falls

Conservatory, Inniskillin and Reif Wineries, Fort Erie, and—if gambling's your game—a casino with 2,700 slot machines and 140 gaming tables.

NIAGARA-ON-THE-LAKE

Niagara-on-the-Lake is one of the best preserved and prettiest 19th-century villages in North America. As host of the Shaw Festival, the town arranges a series of plays written by George Bernard Shaw and his contemporaries. Informal talks precede or follow each performance. The festival takes place every summer from mid-April to the end of October. Away from the festival, you can stroll along Queen Street, take a tour (with tastings) to the nearby wineries, visit Fort George National Historic Park, or take a jet boat in summer down the river to get a close-up view of the canyon. The Welland Canal and the village of Jordan are other places to visit in the vicinity.

INFORMATION

Niagara-on-the-Lake
Distance 80 miles
Travel time 1½ hours
🚌 Public Transit Greyhound ☎ 416/367-8747 or 1/800-661-8747 to St. Catharine's then Charter-ways ☎ 905/688-9600
🚆 VIA Rail ☎ 416/366-8411 or 1/800-561-8630 to St. Catharine's or Niagara Falls
➕ Off map to south
🛈 Niagara-on-the-Lake Chamber of Commerce ✉ 153 King Street (Box 1043), ON L0S 1J0 ☎ 905/468-4263

Niagara-on-the-Lake 21

WHAT'S ON

January	International Boat Show, Exhibition Place.
February	Winterfest, various venues.
March	Canadian Music Festival, various venues. St. Patrick's Day Parade (March 17).
April	Baseball season (to Oct), SkyDome.
May	Milk International Children's Festival (► 57), Harbourfront ☎ 416/973-3000
June	Toronto International Dragon Boat Race Festival, Centre Island. Benson & Hedges Symphony of Fire Fireworks Festival, Ontario Place. Du Maurier Downtown Jazz Festival ☎ 416/928-2033
July	Fringe of Toronto Theatre Festival ☎ 416/534-5919 Canada Day Celebration (July 1). Molson Indy Car Race, Exhibition Place ☎ 416/872-4639 Caribana Carnival, citywide ☎ 416/465-4884
August	Canadian National Exhibition and Canadian International Air Show at Exhibition Place ☎ 416/393-6000 Du Maurier Ltd. Open Tennis Championship, National Tennis Centre.
September	Bell Canadian Open, Glen Abbey Golf Club, Oakville ☎ 905/844-1800 Toronto International Film Festival, citywide ☎ 416/967-7371
October	Toronto Maple Leafs begin hockey season at the Air Canada Centre (► 55).
November	Royal Agricultural Winter Fair and Royal Horse Show, Exhibition Place ☎ 416/393-6400
December	Cavalcade of Lights in front of City Hall. First Night Celebration of the Arts at Harbourfront Centre.

TORONTO's
top 25 sights

The sights are shown on the maps on the inside front cover and inside back cover, numbered **1–25** from west to east across the city

ROYAL BOTANICAL GARDENS

INFORMATION

- ✚ Off map to southwest
- ✉ 680 Plains Road West, Burlington
- ☎ 905/527-1158
- 🕐 Outdoor gardens daily 9:30–dusk. Mediterranean Garden daily 9:30–6. Closed Jan 1
- 🍴 Café ☎ 905/529-2920
- 🚗 Take Queen Elizabeth Way to Hwy 403 (Hamilton). Exit at Hwy 6 North and follow signs to Royal Botanical Gardens Centre
- ♿ Very good
- 💷 Moderate, inexpensive in winter
- ❓ Festivals throughout year—lilac, cherry blossom, rose, iris, herb…

If you are wondering what hedge to plant, come and view the 120 varieties in this 2,690-acre botanical garden exhibiting 40,000 recorded plants. A bonus is provided by the gardens' several nature sanctuaries linked by 20 miles of trails.

Colors and scents The Mediterranean Greenhouse in the RBG Centre is at its best from January to May when bougainvillea, jasmine, mimosas, oranges, lemons, and spring bulbs all bloom. Annuals blossom in the Hendrie Park garden from June to October along with 3,000 roses. Hendrie's specialty gardens include a shade garden and others devoted to scented and medicinal plants. The Laking Garden has perennials, more than 500 varieties of iris, herbaceous and tree peonies (both the iris and peony flower in June), and a heritage garden. The Rock Garden, with its ponds and waterfalls, dazzles in spring when 125,000 bulbs burst into bloom, followed by flowering cherries. June brings a brilliant display of azaleas. Enjoy this garden from the terrace of the Tea House restaurant.

Trees and wilderness The Arboretum shelters 800 varieties of lilac in the romantic lilac dell—one of the largest collections anywhere—with magnolias, dogwoods, and rhododendrons adding to the magnificence. Those hedges are here, as well as an A-to-Z "library" of shrubs, a local wild flower garden, and a sea of Ontario trees and shrubs. At the Teaching Garden observe how to create different environments in a small back garden, smell the fragrances of herbs, and consider edible ornamentals. The gardens protect a wilderness of high cliffs, ravines, and wetlands where deer forage, foxes and coyotes hunt, and blue herons fish. Sanctuaries include Hendrie Valley, Rock Chapel, and Cootes Paradise.

2

McMichael Collection

Known as the Group of Seven, the artists took their easels north and painted what they saw. In doing so, they revealed the northern wilderness to Canadians and the rest of the world. Today, their revolutionary works are displayed here in an appropriate woodland setting.

Artist by artist The permanent collection chronicles the development of the Group of Seven. The works of each are hung together so that viewers can see how each artist evolved. All the favorites are here: the brilliantly colored canvases of Lake Superior by A. Y. Jackson; Algonquin Park as seen by Tom Thomson; the rural villages depicted by A. J. Casson; the Killarney Provincial Park rendered by Franklin Carmichael; the starkly beautiful icebergs captured by Lawren Harris; portraits of British Columbia by F. H. Varley; and the rendering of northwestern forests and Native Canadian villages by Emily Carr. Less familiar followers of the school include J. W. Beatty, Charles Comfort, George Pepper, Kathleen Daly, Lilias Torrence Newton, and Thoreau MacDonald. In one gallery, a series of paintings portrays the Seven working outdoors. The most appealing depicts Franklin Carmichael sketching at Grace Lake in 1935. It shows him from behind as he perches in front of an easel wrapped in a heavy parka with the hood peaking at the top of his head.

First Nations and Inuit art Paintings, drawings, prints, and sculptures by contemporary Native American and Inuit artists—Norval Morrisseau, Daphne Odjig, Alex Janvier, Bill Reid—are displayed in changing shows drawn from the permanent collection. Fine Inuit sculptures and other crafts complete this excellent collection.

HIGHLIGHTS

- Emily Carr's *Corner of Kitwancool Village*
- Lawren Harris's *Mt Lefroy*
- J. E. H. MacDonald's *Forest Wilderness*
- A. Y. Jackson's *First Snow*
- Tom Thomson's *Wood Interior, Winter*
- Arthur Lismer's *Bright Land*
- F. H. Varley's *Night Ferry*
- First Nations art
- Inuit sculpture

INFORMATION

- Off map to northwest
- Islington Avenue, Kleinburg
- 905/893-1121
- Apr–Oct: daily 10–5. Nov–Mar: Tue–Sun 10–4.
- Restaurant, cafeteria
- Good
- Moderate
- Canada's Wonderland (➤ 26)
- Weekend tours at 1PM; special events

Above: A.Y. Jackson, The Red Maple *(1914) detail*

CANADA'S WONDERLAND

INFORMATION

- Off map to northwest
- 9580 Jane Street Vaughan. Take Highway 400 to Rutherford Road
- 905/832-7000
- May: daily 10–6. Early Jun: daily 10–8. Mid-Jun–Labour Day: daily 10–10. Sep–2nd week in Oct: Sat, Sun 10–8. Closed winter
- Many outlets
- Yorkdale or York Mills and then GO bus
- Few
- Very expensive (One Price Passport). Additional fees for karts, theater, mini-golf, Xtreme Skyflyer
- McMichael Collection (► 25), Black Creek Pioneer Village (► 27)
- Special events from fireworks to video dance fests

Rollercoaster riders revel in this park, for it contains ten coasters—enough to satisfy even the most jaded addict. The park has more than 50 rides and 180 attractions—adding new thrillers every year to keep the locals coming back.

Gut-wrenchers The park's latest hair-raiser is The Fly, an update of the Wild Mouse, a coaster that drops riders 50 feet on some of the loops. Another thriller is the daredevil Drop Zone, which takes riders 230 feet up and then drops them, in an open carriage, in a 60mph free fall. A further heart-stopping experience awaits you at the Xtreme Skyflyer, which elevates you to 150 feet and then delivers the combined thrills of skydiving and hang-gliding (there's an additional charge for this). Still, the rollercoasters remain the perennial favorites: the looping inverted Top Gun, a standing loop version called Sky Rider, a wooden coaster for nostalgia seekers, and several other metal coasters.

Water plus Splashworks, the 20-acre water park, is another major attraction. It offers an extra-large wave pool generating white caps, and 16 different water slides, including one with eight stories and another involving a 400-foot drop in the dark. There's also a wacky aquatic jungle gym for small children.

Less strenuous If you tire of flipping your stomach, then there are plenty of other things to do: the Kingswood Theatre, where musical groups entertain; encounters with ferocious monsters in a 3-D movie ride at the Paramount Action F/X Theatre; street entertainment by Hanna-Barbera characters and Nickleodeon's Rugrats in Kidzville; and batting cages and mini golf. At Speed City Raceway, there are two-seater karts.

BLACK CREEK PIONEER VILLAGE

This "living history" park re-creates 19th-century Ontario village life as authentically as possible. Leave behind the stresses of modern times and take a step back in the past to find out what existence was like in a pioneer community.

Family farm Black Creek is built around the Stong family farm—their first log house (1816), smokehouse and barn (1825), and a second clapboard home that they built in 1832. Even the sheep and hogs are authentic, since they are imported English breeds that would have been familiar to the 19th-century pioneers.

Village life The village consists of some 30 mid-19th-century buildings. Wandering along the pathways and boardwalks between them, you seem to slip into a slower pace of life, one established by the horse rather than the car. Seeds are sold at the Laskay Emporium store, along with old-fashioned candy and handcrafted brooms made in the village. Half Way House, so called because it stood halfway between York and Scarborough, is a stagecoach tavern. Every day loaves are baked here in the old hearth oven. These convincing surroundings are brought to life by the artisans who take delight in passing on their skills and knowledge. The cooper hunches over the barrel stove compressing staves to make watertight barrels and pails held together without a single nail. Others demonstrate tinsmithing, weaving, cabinetmaking, blacksmithing, clock-making, and printing. Dickson's Hill School is a one-room schoolhouse that nevertheless has separate entrances for boys and girls. The gardens include a herb garden with 42 familiar herbs, the weaver's dye garden containing plants like blood-root (red), sunflowers (yellow), and woad (blue), and the doctor's medicinal garden.

HIGHLIGHTS

- Coopering
- Tinsmithing
- Flour milling
- Pioneer gardens
- Laskay Emporium and post office
- Half Way House

INFORMATION

- ✚ Off map to north
- ✉ 1000 Murray Ross Parkway, North York
- ☎ 416/736-1733
- ⏰ May–Aug: daily 10–5. Sep: Wed–Sun 10–5. Oct–Nov: Wed–Sun 10–4:30. Dec: daily 10–4:30
- 🍴 Restaurant, coffee cart
- 🚇 Jane subway and 35B bus; Finch subway and 60B, 60D and 60E bus
- ♿ Few
- 💲 Moderate
- ↔ Canada's Wonderland (➤ 26)

Above: a cooper at work
Below: feeding the pigs

ONTARIO PLACE

INFORMATION

➕ F10

✉ 955 Lake Shore Boulevard West, between Dufferin and Strachan Avenue

☎ 416/314-9811 or 314-9900

🕐 Mid-May–Labour Day: daily 10:30–midnight. Most attractions close at dusk

🍽 Many restaurants and snack bars

🚌 Bus 121 Front-Esplanade from Union Station, or streetcar 511 Bathurst–Exhibition Place

♿ Good

💲 Expensive

↔ Fort York (➤ 29)

❓ Special events, including fireworks

The futuristic glass complex of Ontario Place

This weird and wonderful waterfront recreation complex, a futuristic-looking creation of the 1970s, has a lagoon ambience that appeals to visitors of all ages and types.

Always up-to-date Ontario Place is spread over three man-made islands and adds up to a 96-acre park with rides, attractions, top-name performers, IMAX films, stage shows, and restaurants. The original Ontario Place, designed in 1971 by architects Craig-Zeidler-Strong of Toronto, won many awards for excellence. To keep it up to date, new attractions are added every year.

Water, water everywhere At Children's Village, an imaginative creative play park, youngsters can scramble over rope bridges, bounce on an enormous trampoline, squirt water pistols and garden hoses at each other, and enjoy the entertainment on the Festival Stage. The two waterslides, the Pink Twister and the Purple Pipeline, are not far behind in popularity and neither is the flume ride called Wilderness Adventure Ride. For daredevils there is the Hydrofuge, a tubular waterslide which sends riders speeding at 30mph into a spinning bowl before depositing them into a six-foot-deep landing pool. Sea Trek is a deep-sea submarine simulator; or you can shoot the rapids on the Rush River attraction.

Entertainment too Other attractions are inside eye-catching steel and glass structures ("pods"). The Lego Pod has huge Lego creations, while the Thrill Zone Pod features many simulator experiences and video games. The Molson Amphitheatre seats 16,000 (including 7,000 on the lawns) for stellar summer performances. The Atlantis Complex contains several restaurants and lounges and features an evening dance club.

6

FORT YORK

A visit to this complex of buildings sandwiched between the railroad tracks and the highway will give you a historic jolt back to 1813 when muddy York was a rough-and-ready imperial outpost.

Fort York and the White House On April 27, 1813, during the War of 1812, 2,700 Americans stormed ashore from Lake Ontario. They drove out the troops at Fort York and set fire to Government House and the Parliament Buildings. In 1814, in retaliation, the British occupied Washington and burned the president's residence. According to Canadian legend, the Americans covered up the blackened walls with white paint, and from then on it was called the White House, but the Americans say it was named for the stone.

Military memorabilia John Graves Simcoe built a garrison on the site of Fort York in 1793. The fort was strengthened in 1811 (the west wall and circular battery date from that time) and, shortly after the events of 1813, the British rebuilt it; most of the fort's buildings date from that time. The officers' quarters (1815) have been meticulously furnished to reflect the late 1830s. The Blue Barracks has exhibits on Canadian military history from the War of 1812 to the trench warfare of World War I. In Blockhouse 2, which served as 160-man barracks, a video and dioramas relate the history of the fort. The East Magazine (1814) displays some of the 12,000 artifacts retrieved, documenting the officers' daily life—buckles, heel plates, buttons, baleen tweezers. The Stone Magazine (1815) provided bombproof storage for 900 barrels of gunpowder within its six-foot-thick walls.

HIGHLIGHTS

- ● Officers' Quarters
- ● Stone Magazine

INFORMATION

- ✚ G9
- ✉ Garrison Road, off Fleet Street between Bathurst Street and Strachan Avenue
- ☎ 416/392-6907
- 🕐 Mon–Fri 10-5; Sat–Sun 12–5
- 🚊 Bathurst 511 streetcar
- ♿ Few
- 🍴 Moderate
- ↔ SkyDome (➤ 35), CN Tower (➤ 36), The Pier (➤ 54)
- ❓ Tours by interpreters in period costume. Jul–Aug: drills, musket and cannon firing, fife and drum music

Casa Loma

HIGHLIGHTS

- Great Hall
- Oak Room
- Conservatory

INFORMATION

- ✚ H5
- ✉ 1 Austin Terrace at Davenport and Spadina Road
- ☎ 416/923-1171
- 🕐 House daily 9:30–4. Gardens May–Oct: 9:30–4
- 🍴 Café
- Ⓜ Dupont
- ♿ Good
- 💵 Moderate
- ❓ Self-guided tour; garden talks

The Great Hall at Casa Loma

A mixture of 17th-century Scottish baronial and 20th Century Fox, Casa Loma is a rich man's folly on a grand scale. It cost $3.5 million to build, yet due to the changes in real estate, only ten years later was valued at an astonishing $27,305.

Splendor Canadian-style A magnificent and whimsical place with its Elizabethan chimneys, Rhenish turrets, underground tunnels, and secret passageways, Casa Loma is Sir Henry Pellatt's fantasy of what constituted European aristocratic splendor. Between 1911 and 1914 Pellatt created this fantasy home, importing Scottish stone-masons and Italian woodcarvers to embellish it, then spending an additional $1.5 million furnishing the 98 rooms. The results are grand. A hammerbeam ceiling covers the 66-foot-high Great Hall; three artisans took three years to carve the paneling in the Oak Room; splendid bronze doors lead into the marble conservatory crowned with a stained-glass dome. Modern conveniences and luxuries included an elevator, a private telephone system, marble swimming pool, 10,000-volume library, 15 baths, and 5,000 electric lights. One underground tunnel runs out to the stables, where the horses, stabled amid the luxury of Spanish tile and mahogany, had their names set in 18-carat gold letters at the head of each stall.

The bubble bursts The son of a stockbroker, Pellatt went into the brokerage business after college, and bought huge blocks of stock in the Northwest Land Company and the Canadian Pacific Railway. By 1910 he had amassed $17 million. Still in his 20s, he founded Toronto's first hydroelectric power company, but his wealth evaporated in 1920 when electric power was ruled a public utility. Pellatt was eventually to decline into poverty, and died penniless in 1939.

KENSINGTON MARKET

Throughout its history, Kensington Market has been the domain of the major immigrant group of the decade. Once Jewish, then Portuguese, today it is more Asian/Caribbean than anything else. Saturday is the busiest day.

Multiethnic tastes There is no central market square, just a series of narrow streets—notably Kensington and Augusta Avenues and Baldwin Street—lined with stores selling all kinds of provisions. From Spadina Avenue turn down St. Andrews Street to Kensington Avenue, then turn right. There are several West Indian grocery stores on this street, selling yucca, sugarcane, plantains, papaya, mangoes, and other tropical items. Don't miss Mendel's Creamery selling smoked fish, herring, cheeses, and gigantic dill pickles. Global Cheese, next door, offers an around-the-world education in cheeses. Portuguese fish markets, like Medeiro's, line much of Baldwin Street. Outside each storefront, boxes are piled high with flat, stiff dried cod.

Snacking Wonderful aromas waft out of the Baldwin Street Bakery, which is worth a stop for a croissant or some other snack. Other stores on Baldwin display all kinds of grains, beans, nuts, and fruits. Pick up an energizing snack of dried papaya, mango, pineapple, or apricots at Salamanca, along with some pecans or filberts from Casa Acoreana. Around the corner, on Augusta Avenue, go into Perola Supermarket to see the cassava and the myriad varieties of peppers—ancho, arbol, pasilla, and more—and the many medicinal roots that are for sale here. Piñatas hang from the ceiling, and in the back of the store you'll find a woman selling tasty *pupusas*, which are meat- and cheese-filled *tamales*.

HIGHLIGHTS

- Mendel's Creamery
- Global Cheese
- Medeiro's Fish Market
- Baldwin Street Bakery
- Salamanca
- Casa Acoreana
- Perola Supermarket

INFORMATION

- H7
- Bounded by Spadina and Augusta Avenues between College and St. Andrews
- Stores open normal hours
- Dundas or College streetcar
- Chinatown (➤ 50)

Vendors displaying their goods

9

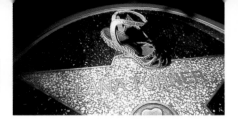

BATA SHOE MUSEUM

Imelda Marcos would be in her element at this museum. You will never look down at your shoes in quite the same way again after viewing these extraordinary displays of footwear past and present.

HIGHLIGHTS

- Mold of first steps taken by *Homo sapiens* 3,700,000 years ago
- 4,500-year-old wooden sandals
- 2,000-year-old espadrilles
- 500-year-old rawhide moccasins belonging to a Mayan boy sacrifice
- 3-inch "gin lien" for bound feet
- French 19th-century chestnut crushing boots

INFORMATION

- H6
- 327 Bloor Street
- 416/979-7799
- Tue–Wed, Fri–Sat 10–5; Thu 10–8; Sun noon–5
- St. George
- Excellent
- Moderate
- University of Toronto (➤ 33), ROM (➤ 39), George R. Gardiner Museum (➤ 40), Yorkville (➤ 51)
- Lectures, workshops, storytelling programs

More than just shoes The main permanent exhibit traces the history of shoes from the first footprint made 3.7 million years ago in Tanzania to the extraordinary shoes of today. The sheer variety of beautiful and truly striking footwear is amazing. Each display is set against an appropriate series of cutouts reflecting the particular period or geographic location. There are all kinds of ceremonial shoes: leather sandals with gilded images worn by the King of Kumasi in Ghana for state occasions; wedding shoes from various cultures; and lacquered and painted shoes worn to Shinto shrines in Japan. The museum is a goldmine of little-known facts; for instance, that Elizabeth I is in part responsible for the foot problems caused by high heels because it was she who popularized them in an attempt to make herself appear taller. The style was limited to the elite, hence the term "well-heeled." Toe-length was another important indicator of social status; in England, in the mid-14th century, anyone earning under 40 livres was not allowed to wear pointed toes, a nobleman could wear shoes with toes 24 inches long, and a prince could wear shoes with toes of any length. The display culminates in "The Shoes of the Stars"—Picasso's mock zebra lace-ups, Elton John's 12-inch-high platform shoes, and the sandals worn by former Canadian premier Pierre Trudeau when he was hiking around the world.

Right: Elton John's platforms

University of Toronto

Important scientific discoveries have emanated from this venerable institution, most notably insulin. The university also numbers many now world-famous names among its past students and teachers.

Famous alumni and remarkable research Founded in 1827, this is Canada's largest university with more than 50,000 students. The university's scientific achievements include pioneering work that led to the development of the laser; the first electronic heart pacemaker; and the discovery of the gene responsible for the most severe form of Alzheimer's Disease. Notable alumni include authors Margaret Atwood, Farley Mowat and Stephen Leacock; figures from the movie world Atom Egoyan, Norman Jewison, and Donald Sutherland; opera singers Teresa Stratas and Maureen Forrester; and prime ministers Mackenzie King and Lester Pearson.

Gothic and modern Stroll around the downtown main St. George campus to view the mixture of architecture. On Hoskin Avenue see Wycliffe and Trinity Colleges, the first a monument of redbrick Romanesque Revival and the second a Gothic complex with chapel and eye-catching gardens. Around the corner on Devonshire Place, Massey College is a 1960s building; writer Robertson Davies was Master here for many years. The heart of the university is Hart House, consciously modeled on Magdalen College, Oxford, with its impressive Gallery Grill. See the collection of Canadian art in the Justina M. Barnicke Art Gallery in the west wing. Just south of Hart House is the Romanesque Revival University College, with an arts center (► 54) in the Laidlaw Building. King's College Circle passes by several other stately university buildings.

DID YOU KNOW?

- Engineering pioneer Ursula Franklin is a professor emeritus
- Immunologist and virologist Dr. Tak Mak, the first to clone a lymph cell gene, is on the faculty
- The university's Dr. Lap Chee Tsui was on the team that discovered the cystic fibrosis gene
- More than 50 percent of undergraduates are women
- The Royal Ontario Museum, the Canadian Opera Company, and the Toronto Symphony all started there
- Hypersonic flight (Mach 5) was pioneered here with the first airplane powered by microwaves

INFORMATION

- ⊞ J6, J7
- ⊠ West of Queen's Park
- ☎ 416/978-5000
- 🍴 Gallery Grill in Hart House and numerous cafeterias in campus buildings
- ⊚ Museum or Queen's Park
- ⊟ College Street streetcar
- ♿ Good
- 🎟 Free
- ↔ Royal Ontario Museum (► 39), George R. Gardiner Museum (► 40), Ontario Parliament Buildings (► 41)
- ❓ Tours year round. Special tours Jun–Aug

11

HARBOURFRONT ANTIQUES MARKET

HIGHLIGHTS

- Connoisseur Antiques
- Blue Antiques
- Caspian Pearl
- Pam Ferrazzutti
- Heritage Jewellery & Arts
- Yank Azman
- Sphinx

INFORMATION

- ✚ H9
- ✉ 390 Queens Quay West at Spadina
- ☎ 416/260-2626
- 🕒 Summer: Tue–Sat 10–6; Sun 8–6. Winter: Tue–Sun 10–6
- 🍴 Café
- 🚇 Union then Harbourfront LRT; Spadina and bus 77
- ♿ Good
- 🎟 Free
- ↔ Harbourfront (➤ 42)

This covered market trades in all types of antiques, including art nouveau and art deco pieces, 18th-century French items, and 20th-century kitsch. It is best to come on weekends, when more than 100 dealers are usually at their stands.

Choice pickings whatever the weather This is a great market for browsing in comfort in all weathers. The quality of the merchandise is good and the prices fair, when you allow for discounts against the Canadian dollar. There are kitschy posters, military models, chandeliers, thimbles, old plates, silver daggers, walking sticks, Elvis buttons, vintage telephones and cameras, maplewood furniture, blunderbusses and other firearms, clocks, toy soldiers, fascinating jewelry, and scientific and medical instruments.

A few places to start looking Connoisseur Antiques has some elegant Louis XV and XVI furniture, impressive ormolu mirrors and chandeliers, as well as jewelry, porcelain, and paintings. Grand Victorian majolica vases, chargers, and jardinières, plus vintage sporting items, can be found at Pam Ferrazzutti. For whimsical objects and theatrical props go to Yank Azman; he has scientific and medical instruments, sporting goods, and hand luggage too. Caspian Pearl has wonderful jewelry along with tent tassels, miniature paintings, and other Middle Eastern decorative objects. To find art nouveau and art deco jewelry as well as objets d'art, head for the Heritage Jewellery & Arts. If you can raise your eyes from the merchandise there's always a chance you might see a celebrity figure or two—Goldie Hawn, Jane Fonda, Madonna and Whoopi Goldberg have been known to visit the market.

SkyDome

The home of the Blue Jays in downtown Toronto is so revolutionary in design that it has become an attraction with an organized tour. It is one of the few stadiums in the world where you can sit in a hotel suite with a grandstand view of the field.

Engineering feat Numbers help to illustrate the great engineering feat represented by the stadium. The largest ever built, it has a fully retractable roof and required much engineering ingenuity in its design and execution. The 12,000-ton roof covers nearly eight acres and there are 250,000 roof bolts, yet it can be opened in 20 minutes thanks to the ingenious steel track and the trucks driven by 10-horsepower motors. Although the tour film is cloying beyond belief, it does offer a glimpse of what it was like to build this vast structure. When the camera pans up the girders, the height of them is scary.

Tour topics On the tour, visitors are given a mass of statistics about the astroturf, and how long it takes for it all to be stuck together; you visit one of the astronomically expensive corporate skyboxes and take a look at the broadcast/press facilities. The stadium incorporates an 11-story hotel where the rooms have great views facing onto the field and can be rented on game nights for upwards of $800. The Toronto Blue Jays Clubhouse is off limits to visitors, except occasionally during the March break, but you can have a peek (when events permit) at the visiting team's dressing room. The Toronto Argonauts (Canadian football) also play here, as does the Blizzard soccer team; other entertainment ranges from circuses to pop concerts and ice shows.

HIGHLIGHTS

- Retractable roof
- Video that explains the stadium's construction
- Corporate skyboxes
- Press facilities
- Dressing room
- Hotel overlooking the field

The Audience *by Michael Snow*

INFORMATION

- ✚ H9–J9
- ✉ 1 Blue Jays Way
- ☎ 416/341-2770. For Blue Jays game tickets ☎ 416/341-1234 well ahead
- 🍴 Restaurants, cafés, and snackbars
- Ⓤ Union Station
- 🚋 Front Street streetcars
- ♿ Very good
- 💷 Expensive
- ↔ CN Tower (➤ 36)
- ❓ Tours

35

CN TOWER

HIGHLIGHTS

- Glass floor
- View from observation deck
- SkyPod
- Edge Arcade
- Maple Leaf Theatre
- Simulator rides
- The ride up

INFORMATION

- J9
- 301 Front Street West
- 416/360-8500
- Jan–early spring: Sun–Thu 9AM–10PM, Fri–Sat 9AM–11PM. Spring–Dec: daily 8AM–11PM
- 360 Restaurant 416/362-5411, Horizons, Marketplace Cafe
- Union Station
- Front Street streetcar
- Very good
- Observation deck expensive; games expensive
- SkyDome (➤ 35)

The CN Tower is Toronto's trademark. Like San Francisco's TransAmerica and Seattle's Space Needle, it was derided at first but ultimately embraced by citizens and visitors alike. It is still the world's tallest free-standing tower.

On a clear day It's certainly a stomach-churning experience to rocket at 20 feet per second in glass-fronted elevators to the SkyPod's observation deck. On arrival, you step out onto a small glass floor and peer down at the ground, 1,135 feet below. From the outdoor observation deck, on a clear day, you can see the mist of Niagara Falls on the opposite side of the lake. You can also take the elevator another 33 stories up to the SkyPod at 1,463 feet. The tower has attracted assorted record-seekers—including Ashrita Furman, who bounced on his pogo stick up the 1,967 steps to the SkyPod roof in 57 minutes and 43 seconds.

Shopping and other entertainments Down at the base of the tower there's hands-on action in the Edge Arcade, featuring simulated game experiences like Indy Racing and Alpine Racer. The Ultimate Roller Coaster takes you on a pitch-and-roll ride, while the Easy Glide Canadian Panorama is a more sedate trip though the Rockies. The Maple Leaf Theatre shows a 22-minute film "Momentum-Images" of Canada. The Marketplace offers varied shopping. Before you go up the tower, check out the touch screen kiosks that tell the story of how it was built. Here too, let the daredevil in you imagine the thrill of bungee jumping from the observation level or walking on a tightrope to neighboring skyscrapers.

14

ART GALLERY OF ONTARIO

Boldly painted to great effect, this is a showcase for Canadian and European art: there is also a superb special Henry Moore collection. The whole gallery is arranged around the historic Grange (► 38).

Canada's best The Canadian artists known as the Group of Seven (► 12, 25) had their first show here in 1920, and the galleries displaying their works are exceptional. See Tom Thomson's *The West Wind* (1917), J. E. H. MacDonald's *Falls, Montreal River* (1920), Lawren Harris's *Above Lake Superior* (1922), and Emily Carr's *Indian Church* (1929). Other Canadian galleries trace the development of Canadian art. Look for Joseph Legare's *The Fire in the Saint Jean Quarter Seen Looking Westward* (1845), James Wilson Morrice's *Gibraltar* (1913), Paul Emile Borduas' *Woman with Jewel* (1945), Paterson Ewen's *Coastal Trip* (1974), Joanne Tod's *Similac* (1992), and Jeff Wall's *The Goat* (1989). Don't miss the Inuit galleries, with displays of sculptures, prints, and drawings.

Henry Moore collection The Henry Moore Sculpture Centre, which opened in 1974, houses one of the largest public collections of his works. A series of color photographs show many of Moore's major works in their original locations.

From the Old World Of European art, most noteworthy are the 17th-century works by Luca Giordano, Antoine Coypel, Jean-Baptiste Jouvenet, and Jusepe de Ribera, as well as some fine Florentine baroque bronzes. The gallery has works by Picasso, Dufy, Modigliani, Brancusi, Gauguin, Chagall, Barbara Hepworth, Naum Gabo, and the surrealists. There are also collections of photographs, prints, and drawings, and an outstanding film archive.

HIGHLIGHTS

- Group of Seven galleries
- Inuit collection
- Henry Moore Sculpture Centre

INFORMATION

- ➕ J8
- ✉ 317 Dundas Street West
- ☎ 416/979-6648
- 🕐 Summer: Tue–Fri noon–9; Sat–Sun 10–5:30. Winter: Wed–Fri noon–9; Sat–Sun and holidays 10–5:30
- 🍴 Agora Restaurant
- 🚇 St. Patrick
- 🚋 Dundas streetcar
- ♿ Very good
- 💲 Moderate
- ↔ Chinatown (► 50), Museum for Textiles (► 54), Eaton Centre (► 70)
- ❓ Tours, lectures, films, concerts

15

THE GRANGE

HIGHLIGHTS

- Dining room
- Bedrooms
- Breakfast parlor
- Music room
- Kitchen
- Fire in the hearth
- Whatever has come out of the oven on the day

INFORMATION

- ✚ J8
- ✉ 317 Dundas Street West
- ☎ 416/977-0414
- ◑ Winter: Wed noon–9; Thu–Sun noon–4. Summer: Tue noon–4; Wed noon–9; Thu–Sun noon–4
- 🍴 Restaurant at Art Gallery of Ontario
- Ⓢ St. Patrick
- ⊟ Dundas streetcar
- ♿ Few
- 💲 Moderate
- ↔ AGO (➤ 37), Chinatown (➤ 50), Eaton Centre (➤ 70)
- ❓ Self-guided tours

This house museum gives an insight into an era when the city was a much less liberal place, ruled by a handful of power-mongers, referred to collectively as The Family Compact. It offers a fascinating glimpse of how one of these families lived.

The Boulton family home   When Harriette Dixon Boulton Smith died in 1909, she bequeathed the Grange and its 6 acres of parkland to the then homeless Art Gallery of Ontario (➤ 37). It was originally the home of D'Arcy Boulton, Jr. who built it in 1817 on 100 acres. The Boultons were members of the ruling elite and the house became a center of social and political life. D'Arcy occupied a series of government positions and his son, William Henry, was Mayor of Toronto four times. When William Henry died, his widow married Goldwin Smith, journalist and professor of Modern History at Oxford, who entertained lavishly. Among the visitors were Edward, the Prince of Wales, and Winston Churchill.

Upper-class Toronto in 1840   The house is decorated to represent life as it was in the mid-19th century and the contents of each room are described on paddleboards. Downstairs, the pier table in the dining room provoked criticism of the family because it was made in the United States, while the pole fire screen in the parlor guarded fashionably pallid complexions against a rosy glow. Upstairs there are two bedrooms and a large music room, where parties and balls were held. The most interesting part of the residence is the servants' quarters. Down here a fire burns in the hearth adjacent to the bake oven. Here, too, are some historical exhibits documenting the wealth of most of the other members of The Family Compact.

Above: the Grange's enormous kitchen

ROYAL ONTARIO MUSEUM

Among the 40 galleries and 6 million objects at the ROM, you'll find dinosaurs, an eerie bat cave, one of the world's foremost Chinese collections, and a remarkable collection of European and Canadian decorative arts.

East and west The T. T. Tsui Chinese galleries display bones used as oracles, bronze vessels, Han jades, and T'ang dynasty earthenware warriors. A Ming tomb is accompanied by a model of a Chinese house (buried in the tomb), while the Levy Court contains traditional room settings from the Ming and Qing dynasties plus a lovely collection of snuff bottles and a fine ceramics gallery. Particularly impressive are the wall paintings and monumental sculptures (12th–16th centuries) in the Bishop White Gallery of Chinese Temple Art. Mummies are the favorites in the Egyptian galleries; pottery, jewelry, sculpture, coins, and glassware fill the Greek and Roman galleries. The Samuel European Galleries exhibit arms and armor, and some exquisite period rooms. The Sigmund Samuel Canadiana gallery showcases Canadian decorative arts. A new gallery of Korean art opened in 1999.

The natural world The Life Sciences Galleries on evolution, insects, mammals, and birds are well conceived. The bird galleries, for instance, include a realistic diorama of the Ontario wetlands, and invite visitors to explore birdsong at several computer terminals. The bat cave is a replica of the St. Clair Cave in Jamaica. The dinosaur galleries contain 13 realistically displayed skeletons. In the gem and gold room don't miss the 2,998-carat blue topaz.

HIGHLIGHTS

- Bishop White Gallery
- The Ming tomb
- Life Sciences Galleries
- Birdsong computer terminals
- Bat cave
- Gem and gold room

INFORMATION

- ✚ J6
- ✉ 100 Queen's Park
- ☎ 416/586-5549 or 586-8000
- ◷ Mon, Wed–Sat 10–6; Tue 10–8; Sun 11–6
- 🍴 JK ROM (➤ 63, lunch only), Etrusco, Druxey's, Cafeteria
- Ⓜ Museum
- ♿ Excellent
- 💷 Expensive
- ↔ Bata Shoe Museum (➤ 32), George R. Gardiner Museum (➤ 40), Yorkville (➤ 51)

A buddha from the T. T. Tsui Chinese Galleries

GEORGE R. GARDINER MUSEUM

HIGHLIGHTS

- Olmec figures
- Smiling figures
- Majolica
- *Commedia dell'arte* figures
- Scent bottles

INFORMATION

- ✠ J6
- ✉ 111 Queen's Park
- ☎ 416/586-8080
- ◷ Tue 10–8; Wed–Sat 10–5; Sun 11–5 (from Victoria Day to Labour Day: Tue 10–7:30)
- Museum
- Very good
- Free (donation requested)
- Bata Shoe Museum (➤ 32), University of Toronto (➤ 33), Royal Ontario Museum (➤ 39), Ontario Parliament Buildings (➤ 41), Yorkville (➤ 51)
- ❓ Tours, lectures

Above: Meso-american exhibits
Right: majolica Madonna and Child

This outstanding display of fine pottery and porcelain, highlighting particular historical periods, was amassed by collectors George and Helen Gardiner. Though small, the museum is diverse enough to provide plenty of interest.

Colorful earthenware   On the first floor is a marvelous collection of pre-Columbian pottery. The figures and vessels date from 3000 BC to the 16th century and range from Mexico to Peru. Among them are some remarkable pieces by the Olmecs, red clay Nayarit figures, Zacatecan-style male statuettes with mushroom-shaped horns, extraordinary smiling figures from Nopiloa, Los Cerros or Isla de Sacrificios, fine orange and plumbate ware of the Mayans, and Aztec objects. The next great period of ceramic art is represented by colorful Italian majolica from the 15th and 16th centuries, and there is a selection of English tin-glazed earthenware, including the familiar blue and white Delftware.

Delicate porcelain   The second floor is devoted entirely to porcelain, including figures by Meissen's famous sculptor-potter Joachim Kändler and some prime examples of Sèvres. English porcelain is well represented, from the early softpaste pieces manufactured at Chelsea and Bow to the later bone china invented by Josiah Spode. The collection also features 120 figures from the *commedia dell'arte*, plus 100 mid-18th-century scent bottles, with examples ranging from early Meissen to highly decorated rococo versions from various sources.

ONTARIO PARLIAMENT BUILDINGS

Most parliamentary institutions deliver great free entertainment, and the Ontario Provincial legislature is no exception, with the 130 members heckling, jeering, and cheering each other as they debate and pass laws. You will either want to join in, or shake your head in disbelief.

Parliamentary session In this impressive four-story chamber the laws affecting 9 million Ontarians are passed. On a dais sits the Speaker who presides over the house. To his right sits the Government, to his left, the Opposition. In the center is the Clerks' table with the mace. Behind the Clerks' table is a smaller table for Hansard record-keepers. On the steps of the dais sit the pages who run errands in the house. Above the speaker is the press gallery. Parliamentary sessions are opened and closed by the Lieutenant Governor. The highlight of any day in the chamber is the question time period when members bombard the premier and cabinet ministers with questions.

Architectural and historical grandeur Even if the house is not sitting you can tour the building, a massive Romanesque revival structure made out of reddish-brown sandstone, opened in 1893. A grand staircase lined with portraits of Ontario premiers sweeps up to the chamber above. An enormous stained-glass ceiling-window lights the East Wing where the premier has his office. The west lobby has mosaic floors, and Italian marble columns in the beaux-arts style, with elaborately carved capitals. On the first floor are historical and regional exhibits, including the original provincial mace which was stolen by the Americans during the 1812 war and only returned under Franklin D. Roosevelt in 1934.

HIGHLIGHTS

- Chamber of the Legislature
- Question time
- Stained-glass ceiling in the East Wing
- The mace

INFORMATION

- ✚ J7
- ✉ Queen's Park
- ☎ 416/325-7500
- 🕐 Sessions Mar–Jun and Sep–Dec
- 🍴 Cafeteria
- 🚇 Queen's Park
- ♿ Good
- 💲 Free
- ↔ Bata Shoe Museum (➤ 32), University of Toronto (➤ 33), Royal Ontario Museum (➤ 39), George R. Gardiner Museum (➤ 40)
- ❓ Tours: Victoria Day–Labour Day daily. Sep–May weekdays only. Reservations needed

19

HARBOURFRONT

HIGHLIGHTS

- Shopping at Queen's Quay
- Art exhibits at the Power Plant
- Craft Studio

INFORMATION

- 🟥 J9
- ✉ 410 Queen's Quay West, Suite 200
- ☎ 416/973-3000 or 973-4600. Tickets: 973-4000
- 🌐 York Quay Information Centre daily 11–8. Queen's Quay daily 10–6

Floating ferries at the harbor entrance

- 🍴 Several
- 🚋 510 streetcar from Union
- ♿ Very good
- 🎟 Free
- ↔ Harbourfront Antiques Market (► 34)
- ❓ Many special events (information at York Quay)

The Harbourfront development is a wonderful example of a waterfront park that is not just a glorified shopping mall. This is a place to spend a whole day— biking, sailing, canoeing, picnicking, watching craftspeople, attending a special event…and even shopping.

Lakefront leisure Start at Queen's Quay where, in an old warehouse building, there is an attractive shopping mall. Several restaurants offer outside dining areas from which to enjoy the waterfront. Walk along the lakeside to York Quay, stopping en route at the Power Plant, a contemporary art gallery, and the Du Maurier Theatre Centre behind it. On York Quay observe artisans glassmaking, pot-throwing, jewelry making, silk-screening, or metal sculpting, and purchase the results in the adjacent store. York Quay's lakefront has a small pond, a children's play area, and the outdoor Molson Place. Across the footbridge is John Quay with several restaurants, while the next quay offers boating (see below). Further along, at the foot of Spadina, is Harbourfront Antiques Market.

Events and activities In good weather, Harbourfront is a wonderful place to relax on the grass or people-watch from one of the waterfront cafés. Alternatively, sail and powerboats can be rented or you can sign up for sailing lessons at the Harbourside Boating Centre ☎ 416/203-3000. Harbourfront offers more than 4,000 events of all sorts, from the Milk International Children's Festival (► 57) to the International Festival of Authors in October.

CITY HALL

Remarkable for its striking design, which shook up Toronto in the early '60s, City Hall could for all intents and purposes be a space station, the council chamber a flying saucer cradled between two semicircular control towers.

Viljo Revell and Nathan Phillips When Mayor Nathan Phillips persuaded the City Council to hold a competition to design a new city hall, the councillors found themselves looking at 520 submissions from 42 countries. Finnish architect Viljo Revell was announced the winner, and his building opened in 1965. The square in front serves as a site for community entertainment; the reflecting pool, where workers eat sandwiches in summer, turns into a skating rink in winter. To the east of City Hall the peace garden contains an eternal flame lit by Pope John Paul II using a flame from the Memorial for Peace at Hiroshima. Near the entrance stands Henry Moore's *Three Way Piece Number Two*, affectionately called *The Archer* by Torontonians.

Open government and municipal art City Hall itself contains several art works. Just inside the entrance, the mural *Metropolis*, by local artist David Partridge, is created from more than 100,000 nails. Continue into the Rotunda and the Hall of Memory, shaped like a sunken amphitheater, where, in the Golden Book, are listed 3,500 Torontonians who died in World War II. At its center rises a large white column that supports the Council Chamber above. The north corridor is lined with a copper and glass mosaic called *Views to the City*, depicting historic panoramic views of the city skyline. From here you can take an elevator up to the Council Chamber which is open to the public every fourth Tuesday.

HIGHLIGHTS

- Viljo Revell's design
- Council Chamber
- Central column in the Hall of Memory
- Hall of Memory
- Nathan Phillips Square
- *Metropolis*
- Henry Moore's *The Archer*
- Peace Garden
- Reflecting pool

INFORMATION

- ✚ J8
- ✉ Queen Street West
- ☎ 416/338-0338
- 🍴 Cafeteria
- 🚇 Queen/Osgoode
- ♿ Very good
- 💲 Free
- ↔ Campbell House (➤ 53), Osgoode Hall (➤ 53)
- ❓ Self-guided tour

City Hall Council Chamber

43

21

THE HOCKEY HALL OF FAME

INFORMATION

- ✚ K9
- ✉ BCE Place at Front and Yonge
- ☎ 416/360-7765
- 🕐 Summer: Mon–Sat 9:30–6 (Thu–Fri until 9:30PM); Sun 10–6. Rest of year: daily Mon–Fri 10–5; Sat 9:30–6; Sun 10:30–5
- 🚇 King and Union
- 🚌 King Street streetcar
- ♿ Very good
- 💵 Very expensive
- ↔ St. Lawrence Market (➤ 46)

Above: the Stanley Cup
Below: hockey sculpture

There's a Canadian saying: first you walk, then you skate. Hockey is to Canadians what football is to Americans and soccer is to the British. It's the one game that most Canadians want to watch and play.

The Stanley Cup and Hall of Fame The jewel of the museum is the Bell Great Hall, once the grand banking hall of the Bank of Montreal. Here the Stanley Cup, North America's oldest professional sports trophy, is displayed in front of the Honoured Members Wall.

Live action At the Rink Zone you will find live shooting booths with sticks and a pail full of pucks; or you can test your goal-keeping skills in front of a TV monitor. At the Impact Zone (for a small charge) you can pad up and play at rookie, professional, or all-star level against Greteky and Messier, who fire sponge pucks at full speed from a video screen.

Eavesdrop on the players In an exact replica of the hallowed dressing room of the Montreal Canadiens, you can spy on the player rituals and routines before the game and listen to Dick Irvin Senior and Junior compare today's sports medicine—laser therapy, ultrasound, and electro massage—with the rub and bandage approach of yesterday. There are memorabilia of teams and players, movie clips of great moments in the game, and displays on the evolution of equipment, from early sticks, like tree branches, to modern aluminum versions, and from early leather masks to the personalized ones (shark teeth, panther jaws) prefered by goalies today.

THE TORONTO ISLANDS

A ferry ride of a mere 20 minutes takes you to this quiet haven of meandering waterways, cycle paths, and bucolic lanes which seems light years away from the city you left behind.

A city retreat Originally a peninsula that was shattered by a storm in 1858, the 14 Toronto islands incorporate 600 acres, crisscrossed by shady paths and laced with quiet waterways and inlets. Until around 1920 there were grand hotels here. Today people come to walk, bike, play tennis, feed the ducks, picnic, sit on the beach, or go boating. There are public swimming areas on Centre and Ward's Island (and a "clothing optional"—nude—beach at Hanlan's Point, only the second one in Canada) but they are often polluted and signposted as such.

Centre, Ward's, and Algonquin These are the main islands. The first is the busiest, with Centreville—an old-fashioned amusement park with an 1890s carousel, a flume ride, antique cars, and a small working farm where children can pet the lambs and ride the ponies. From Centre Island you can take a 45-minute walk to either Hanlan's Point or Ward's Island and catch a return ferry. The other two islands support a community of some 600 residents who live a simple life. On Ward's Island you can walk along the boardwalk to a bridge across the lagoon to Algonquin Island, where there is a spectacular view of the city skyline. The best way to explore is to rent a bike when you get off the ferry and ride from one end of the island to the other, or to take the free tram from Centre Island out to Hanlan's Point.

HIGHLIGHTS

- Centreville
- Hanlan's Point
- View from Algonquin Island

INFORMATION

- ✈ Off map south of harbor.
  Ferries J9–K9
- ☎ Centreville 416/203-0405.
  Ferry 392-8193

Fun on Centreville

- 🍴 Several restaurants/cafés
- 🚃 Harbourfront LRT or Bay 6 and Spadina 77B buses Centreville ferry service operates year round. Winter: every 30–45 minutes morning/evening, and every 2 hours or so during the rest of the day. Summer: service is more frequent
- ♿ Few
- 💲 Inexpensive
- ↔ Harbourfront (➤ 42)
- ❓ Seasonal and other events like Dragon Boat Races

45

St. Lawrence Market

HIGHLIGHTS

- Sausage King
- Carousel Bakery
- Manos Deli
- Future Bakery
- Scheffler's Deli
- Gus Seafood
- Alex Farm
- Caviar Direct

INFORMATION

- K8–K9
- 92 Front Street East
- 416/392-7219
- Tue–Thu 8–6; Fri 8–7; Sat 5–5
- King or Union
- King Street and Front Street streetcars
- Good
- Free
- St. James' Cathedral (► 54)

The lofty 19th-century building that houses this market is entirely worthy of the rich and colorful displays within. This is the place to taste a Canadian peameal bacon sandwich or amass the ingredients for a picnic banquet.

Food lovers' favorites Among the many stalls are a few favorites. At Sausage King you'll find ten or more types of salami—Hungarian, bierwurst, Black Forest wurst, and more. Combine any one with the breads at the Carousel Bakery—sourdough, focaccia, Portuguese cornbread, or pani Calabrese—or grab a peameal bacon sandwich for breakfast (the flavor of the bacon is deliciously enriched by its coating of ground dried peas). Go to Mano's Deli for pastrami or corned beef or Debrezeni sausages on a bun with plenty of kraut, relish, and mustard. Great wheels of cheese can be found at Alex's Farm, from Stilton to Camembert. Any picnic will be enhanced by the chocolate butter tarts, skor brownies, or other pastries sold at Future Bakery. And for good measure, why not throw in some Quebec terrines (rabbit and pistachio, wild boar and apricot, pheasant and mushroom) or pâtés (goose liver, venison), or shrimp and lobster mousse from Scheffler's Deli. Downstairs in the market you'll find Caviar Direct, as well as other stalls offering a variety of foods, including 33 different kinds of rice at Rube's.

Fresh from the fields This historic market is a treat any day, but Saturday is perhaps the best day to come, because that is when the farmers set up stalls at daybreak in the Farmers' Market building across the street, selling fresh produce, preserves, fresh baking, meat, and arts and crafts.

ONTARIO SCIENCE CENTRE

One of the first and still one of the best of its kind, the Ontario Science Centre is a technological extravaganza. Visitors make their way through the museum's different areas, learning as they tune in to more than 800 entertaining interactive exhibits.

High-tech halls Lively and challenging, the Science Centre is divided into 12 halls. Listen to a heart murmur in the Human Body Hall or send a probe into space in the Space Hall. The Sport Hall examines the games people play and the scientific principles involved, and in the Information Highway area, anyone can surf the Net. The Communication Hall deals with the science of human nature and offers games and tests that measure memory, intelligence, and willingness to cooperate. The old adage "You are what you eat" is explored in the Food Hall. A working weather station and a seismograph that lets you create a mini-earthquake are among the big draws in the Earth Hall. There's a working model of the world's first steam engine, and a "bionic woman" with moveable parts in the Technology Hall, and in the Matter, Energy and Change area you can see yourself in infrared. The Science Arcade is filled with whirling, flashing exhibits exploring natural phenomena, while the Question of Truth Hall examines the impact bias, racism, and sexism have had on scientific practice, and the Living Earth Hall focuses on ecology.

Omnimax The other great attraction is the Omnimax Theatre, a 79-foot dome screen with digital wraparound sound that creates the illusion of being in the thick of the movie action. You sit in a tilted-back position and watch a screen 10 times larger than the usual IMAX format.

HIGHLIGHTS

- Human Body Hall
- Space Hall
- Earth Hall
- Omnimax
- Rain Forest

INFORMATION

- ✚ Off map to northeast
- ✉ 770 Don Mills Road, North York at Eglinton
- ☎ 416/696-3127
- 🕐 Aug: daily 10–8. Sep–Jul: daily 10–5
- 🍴 Restaurant, cafeteria
- 🚌 Pape then bus 25 north; Eglinton then bus 34 east; Kennedy then bus 34 west
- ♿ Very good
- 💰 Moderate

TORONTO ZOO

HIGHLIGHTS

- The pavilions, especially Edge of Night in Australasia Pavilion
- Eurasia Outdoor Exhibits
- Americas Pavilion
- Re-created Maya temple
- Africa Pavilion

INFORMATION

- ✚ Off map to northeast
- ✉ 361A Old Finch Avnue, Meadowvale Road, Scarborough
- ☎ 416/392-5900
- ◷ Spring/autumn: daily 9–6. Summer: daily 9–7:30. Winter: daily 9:30–4:30
- 🍴 Two restaurants and four snackbars operated by McDonald's, plus picnic tables
- 🚌 Kennedy and then Scarborough bus 86A going east
- ♿ Very good
- 💲 Expensive
- ❓ "Meet the Keeper" program at various times and venues throughout the day

The 5,000 or so animals at Metro Zoo, representing 459 species, have much more freedom than many in similar institutions. Even their pavilions re-create their natural environment as closely as possible.

Australasia, Eurasia, and the Americas Inspired by the San Diego Zoo, the 710 acres are organized around eight pavilions and nearby outdoor paddocks. Inside each pavilion, a particular habitat and climate is replicated using flora, fauna, and free-flying birds and butterflies. In the Australasia Pavilion you'll see bearded dragons, hairy-nosed wombats, kookaburras, and Tasmanian devils, with kangaroos, wallabies, and emus both inside and outside. The nearby Eurasia Outdoor Exhibits include the Siberian tiger, snow leopard, and yak (plus camel rides). Frighteners in the Americas Pavilion include alligators, black widow spiders, boa constrictors, Mojave desert sidewinders, and pink-toed tarantulas. Polar bears are outdoors, and nearby, at the re-created Maya temple, can be found the jaguar and a flock of flamingos.

Africa and the Indo-Malayan Pavilion Debrazza's and Patas monkeys chatter in the Africa Pavilion, sharing quarters with the Egyptian fruit bat, pygmy hippo, warthog, royal python, and giant Aldabra tortoise. Outdoors, you can go on safari observing zebra, lion, giraffe, ostrich, cheetah, hyena, elephants, white rhinos, and antelope. The orangutan and white-handed gibbon entertain in the Indo-Malaya Pavilion, along with hornbill and reticulated python. Near the pavilion are the Sumatran tigers, Indian rhinoceros, lion-tailed macaque, and, in the Malayan Woods Pavilion, clouded leopard. In the Canadian Domain are a large herd of wood bison plus grizzly bear, wolf, and cougar.

TORONTO's *best*

NEIGHBORHOODS

Shop front at The Beaches

> **See Top 25 Sights for**
> **HARBOURFRONT (➤ 42)**
> **KENSINGTON MARKET (➤ 31)**
> **THE TORONTO ISLANDS (➤ 45)**
> **UNIVERSITY OF TORONTO (➤ 33)**

THE ANNEX
In this residential neighborhood bordering the university, the homes (most built between 1880 and 1920) are populated by professionals, professors and journalists. Residents helped galvanize the opposition to the Spadina Expressway which would have blighted downtown. The strip of Bloor Street on its southern border is lined with coffee houses.
✚ H5–H6, J5–J6 ✉ Avenue Road to Bathurst and Bloor to Dupont ⊙ St. George, Spadina

THE BEACHES
At the eastern end of Queen Street, this is the district favored by baby boomers, attracted to the small-town atmosphere, the boardwalk along the lake, and attractive Victorian homes along tree-shaded streets. Quirky stores, restaurants, cafés, and antique stores add interest to the attractive main street, Queen Street East.
✚ Off map to east ▣ Queen Street East streetcar

CABBAGETOWN
Once described by Canadian author Hugh Garner as "the largest Anglo-Saxon slum in North America," this neighborhood of Victorian homes (between Wellesley and Dundas east of Sherbourne) has been thoroughly gentrified. Rumor has it that it is so named because the front lawns were planted solid with cabbages by the early Irish immigrant residents.
✚ L7 ▣ Dundas, Wellesley or Carlton streetcar

Vibrant Chinatown

CHINATOWN
Sprawling along Dundas and Spadina, the original Chinatown bustles day and night as people shop at stalls displaying brilliant green mustard and bok choy, fresh crabs and live fish, and herbal stores that sell "relaxing tea" and ginseng that costs hundreds of dollars for just one ounce. Today many of the businesses are operated by Thai and Vietnamese.
✚ H7 ⊙ St. Patrick ▣ Dundas streetcar

THE DANFORTH

Across the Don River Ravine east of Bloor, this Greek strip (➤ 18) has become the city's late-night hot spot, where crowds jam the patios of the many bars and restaurants that line the sidewalk. If you come during the day you will find stores specializing in Greek goods, from foodstuffs to figurines.

➕ N6 🚇 Chester, Pape

LITTLE ITALY

A vibrant Italian community thrives along College Street between Euclid and Shaw (➤ 18), where the street lamps bear neon maps of Italy. Old-fashioned cafés with hissing espresso and cappuccino machines operate alongside more modern, fashionable establishments. At night, in particular, the area buzzes with energy.

➕ G7 🚋 College Street streetcar

QUEEN STREET WEST

This is where the hip hang out. It's where cabaret artist Holly Cole began her career and the Bamboo club introduced reggae and salsa to the city. Along this street between Simcoe and Bathurst are the outlets of young Canadian clothing designers, secondhand bookstores, fabric outlets, and junk shops, all mixed up, in a neighborhood that has a very funky edge.

➕ H8–J8 🚇 Osgoode 🚋 Queen Street West streetcar

ROSEDALE

Rosedale is Toronto's most affluent neighborhood, with large and beautiful homes owned by the city's movers and shakers.

➕ K5 🚇 Rosedale

YORKVILLE

Once a village outside the city boundaries, in the 1960s this became Toronto's very own Haight-Ashbury before turning into the fashionable shopping scene that it is today. Designer names cluster in Hazelton Lanes and along Yorkville Avenue, and Bloor and Cumberland Streets.

➕ J6 🚇 Bloor-Yonge, Bay

Yorkville

MODERN BUILDINGS

Raymond Moriyama

Raymond Moriyama (b1929) has given the city several striking buildings, each of which creatively resolves the restrictions of the site, at the same time carefully considering the surrounding environment. At Ontario Science Centre he took into account the ravine and the trees, while the Bata Shoe Museum is a perfect repository for the collection and sympathetic to surrounding buildings.

BCE BUILDING

The whalebone-shaped galleria designed by architects Skidmore, Owings, and Merrill with Bregman & Hamann is superb.
🚩 J9 ☒ 181 Bay Street and Front ☎ 416/364-4693 or 777-6480 🕒 Daily 🍴 Several 🚇 Union ♿ Good 🎫 Free

EATON CENTRE

Enter at the southern end to see the splendor of Ed Zeidler's 866-foot-long galleria and the sculptured flock of 60 Canada geese in flight.
🚩 J8–K8 ☒ Dundas and Yonge to Queen and Yonge ☎ 416/598-8700 🕒 Mon–Fri 10–9; Sat 9:30–6; Sun noon–5 🍴 Several restaurants plus food court 🚇 Dundas or Queen ♿ Very good 🎫 Free

MASSEY COLLEGE

Built 1960–3, and designed by Ron Thom, it features concertina-folded screen walls enclosing a quadrangle and fountain.
🚩 J6 ☒ 4 Devonshire Place 🚇 Queen's Park 🎫 Free

METRO LIBRARY

Architect Raymond Moriyama flooded the library with natural light and gave it a pool and waterfall.
🚩 K6 ☒ 789 Yonge Street ☎ 416/393-7000 🕒 Summer: Mon–Thu 9–8; Fri 9–6; Sat 9–5. Winter: Mon–Thu 10–8; Fri 9–6; Sat 10–5; Sun 1:30–5 🚇 Bloor–Yonge ♿ Very good 🎫 Free

ROYAL BANK PLAZA

The iridescent blaze on a summer day will dazzle your eyes; even when overcast, the distinctive shape of Webb Zerafa Menkes Housden's building will attract your attention.
🚩 J9 ☒ Front and Bay Streets 🍴 Several in concourse 🚇 Union ♿ Very good 🎫 Free

The Roy Thomson Hall

ROY THOMSON HALL

This remarkable, flying-saucer-like creation is by Arthur Erickson; the concert hall is enveloped in a huge glass canopy.
🚩 J8–J9 ☒ 60 Simcoe Street ☎ 416/593-4828 🚇 St. Andrew ♿ Very good 🎫 Free

HISTORIC BUILDINGS

Below: Campbell House

CAMPBELL HOUSE
The 1822 mansion of loyalist and sixth Chief Justice of Upper Canada Sir William Campbell.
➕ J8 ✉ 160 Queen Street West ☎ 416/597-0227
🕐 Mon–Fri 9:30–4:30. Summer only: also Sat–Sun noon–4:30 🚇 Osgoode ♿ Few 💵 Moderate

COLBORNE LODGE
This 1836–7 Regency cottage and the surrounding acreage were donated to the city in 1873. Thus High Park was born (➤ 56).
➕ C 7 ✉ High Park ☎ 416/392-6916 🕐 Jan–mid-Apr: Sat–Sun noon–4. Mid-Apr–early Oct: Tue–Sun noon–5. Early Oct–Dec: Tue–Sun noon–4 🚇 High Park 🚋 No. 501 streetcar ♿ None
💵 Inexpensive

MACKENZIE HOUSE
This humble brick house was bought by friends for William Mackenzie, first mayor of Toronto and leader of the 1837 rebellion. He lived here 1859–61.
➕ K8 ✉ 82 Bond Street ☎ 416/392-6915 🕐 Sat–Sun noon–5. Summer only: Tue–Sun noon–5 🚇 Dundas ♿ Few 💵 Cheap

OLD CITY HALL
Today, Edward James Lennox's massive, Romanesque building houses the provincial courts.
➕ J8 ✉ 60 Queen Street West 🕐 Mon–Fri 9–5 🚇 Queen
♿ Few 💵 Free

OSGOODE HALL
This building (1829) is headquarters of Ontario's legal profession, with an elegant interior and an impressive portrait and sculpture collection.
➕ J8 ✉ 130 Queen Street West ☎ 416/947-3300
🕐 Tours Jul–Aug: Mon–Fri at 1:15 🚇 Osgoode ♿ Few
💵 Free

SPADINA HOUSE
The 1866 house retains its original furnishings and gas lights, plus many decorative objects.
➕ H5 ✉ 285 Spadina Road ☎ 416/392-6910
🕐 Apr–May, Sep: Tue–Fri noon–4; Sat–Sun noon–5. Jun–Aug: daily noon–5. Jan–Mar: Sat–Sun noon–5
🚇 Dupont ♿ Good 💵 Moderate

E. J. Lennox (1855–1933)
Toronto born and educated, Edward James Lennox was one of the city's most influential architects, designing Old City Hall (1889), the west wing of the Provincial Parliament Buildings (1910), and Casa Loma (1914).

Above: Spadina House

MUSEUMS & QUIET CORNERS

Ned Hanlan *tugboat at The Pier*

Two university art galleries

The University of Toronto Art Centre (🞧 J6–J7 ✉ 15 King's College Circle ☎ 416/978-1838) displays the Lillian Malcove Medieval Collection, which includes the 1538 *Adam and Eve* by Lucas Cranach. It also includes some drawings by Picasso, Klee, and Matisse. Hart House has a fine collection of contemporary Canadian art throughout the building and in the Justina M. Barnicke Art Gallery (🞧 J6–J7 ✉ 7 Hart House Circle ☎ 416/978-8398).

MOUNT PLEASANT CEMETERY

Visit the graves of pianist Glenn Gould, the discoverers of insulin Banting and Best, and Prime Minister Mackenzie King. Don't miss the extravagant mausoleums of the Massey and Eaton families.

🞧 K3–L3 ✉ 1643 Yonge Street or 375 Mount Pleasant Road ☎ 416/485-9129 🕐 Daily 8–dusk 🚇 St. Clair ♿ Good 💵 Free

MUSEUM FOR TEXTILES

This gem of a museum has changing exhibitions. Each offers collections that are guaranteed to be aesthetically engaging as well as of anthropological interest.

🞧 J8 ✉ 55 Centre Avenue ☎ 416/599-5321 🕐 Tue–Fri 11–5 (Wed to 8); Sat–Sun noon–5 🚇 St. Patrick ♿ Good 💵 Moderate

THE NECROPOLIS

Beyond the charming porte-cochere and Gothic Revival chapel lie 15 acres of hallowed ground containing many historical figures, including William Lyon Mackenzie and famous oarsman Ned Hanlan.

🞧 L7–M7 ✉ 200 Winchester Street at Sumach Street ☎ 416/923-7911 🕐 Daily 8–dusk 🚇 Castle Frank ♿ Good 💵 Free

THE PIER

This museum tells the story of the lake and the men and ships that plied it. In summer, you can go aboard the *Ned Hanlan* tugboat (1932).

🞧 J9 ✉ 245 Queens Quay ☎ 416/338-7437 🕐 Daily 10–6 🚇 LRT or 510 ♿ Few 💵 Moderate

ST. JAMES' CATHEDRAL

The present building was finished in 1874, but there was an earlier frame building which served as York's first church. In the beautiful interior, note the Tiffany window at the northern end of the east aisle in memory of William Jarvis.

🞧 K8 ✉ 65 Church Street at King ☎ 416/364-7865 🚇 King ♿ Good 💵 Free

SPECTATOR SPORTS & ACTIVITIES

**See Top 25 Sights for
SKYDOME (► 35)**

BASEBALL—THE BLUE JAYS
World Series champions in 1992
and 1993, the team attracts
4 million fans each season.
✚ H9–J9 ✉ 1 Blue Jays Way, Suite 3200
☎ Administration 416/341-1000. Tickets
341-1234 🚇 Union 💷 Very expensive

BASKETBALL—THE RAPTORS
The purple dinosaur that you see
everywhere in the city is the
mascot of Toronto's basketball
team, the Raptors, who appear at
the brand new Air Canada Centre.
✚ H9 ✉ 20 Bay Street, Suite 1702
☎ Administration 416/815-5600
🚇 Union 💷 Very expensive

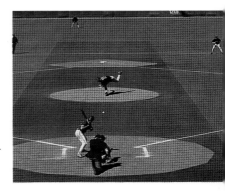

*Blue Jays playing at the
SkyDome*

BIKING
Toronto offers 50 miles of bike routes. The Martin
Goodman Trail runs all along the waterfront. Bikes
can be rented at various venues including the islands.

CANOEING/KAYAKING/SAILING
Queen's Quay Yachting ✉ 283 Queen's Quay West
☎ 416/203-3000 rents out sail and powerboats, and
organizes sailing courses. The Harbourfront Canoe
and Kayak School ✉ 283A Queen's Quay West ☎ 416/203-
2277 rents out kayaks and canoes. Boats can be rented
on the Toronto Islands.

GOLF
The Bell Canadian Open is held on Canada's Labour
Day (first Mon Sep) at Glen Abbey Golf Club in
Oakville. Two worthy metro courses are Humber
Valley ✉ Rexdale ☎ 416/392-2488 and Tam O'Shanter
✉ Birchmount Avenue, Scarborough ☎ 416/392-2547

HOCKEY—THE MAPLE LEAFS
The Leafs played their last game at Maple Leaf
Gardens in February 1999. Now you can witness
Canadians succumbing to hockey fever at Air Canada
Centre. Alas, tickets are almost impossible to obtain.
✚ K7 ✉ 60 Carlton Street ☎ 416/977-1641 🚇 College 💷 Very
expensive

ICE SKATING
In winter, Torontonians head for the rink in front of
City Hall, to Harbourfront, or to Grenadier Pond in
High Park, where a bonfire glows and chestnuts roast.

A trio of sports trivia

1. No matter what others may
tell you, basketball was invented
by a Canadian, James A. Naismith
from Almonte, Ontario in 1891.

2. Before breaking into the
major baseball leagues, Babe
Ruth hit his first home run as a
professional player at a game
played on September 15, 1914,
at Hanlan's Point Stadium on the
Toronto Islands.

3. Lacrosse, not hockey, is
Canada's national game.

GREEN SPACES

See also Top 25 Sights for
METRO ZOO (➤ 48)
ROYAL BOTANICAL GARDENS (➤ 24)

ALLAN GARDENS

The glass-domed Palm House, modeled on the one at Kew Gardens in London, still stands here in radiant Victorian glory.

➕ K7 ✉ Between Jarvis, Sherbourne, Carlton, and Gerrard Streets ☎ 416/392-7288 🕐 Mon–Fri 9–4; Sat–Sun 10–5 🚇 College ♿ Good 🎟 Free

Spring flowers at Edwards Gardens

EDWARDS GARDENS

This formal garden is popular in spring and summer, especially at rhododendron time. Tours leave from the Civic Garden Centre.

➕ Off map to northwest ✉ Lawrence Avenue and Leslie Street ☎ 416/397-1340 🕐 Daily dawn to dusk 🚇 Eglinton and then Leslie or Lawrence bus ♿ Good 🎟 Free

HIGH PARK

This 395-acre park is the city playground. Grenadier Pond becomes a skating rink in winter. In summer, people bike, jog, stroll, picnic, swim in the pool, and play games on the sports fields.

➕ C6–C7 ✉ Bloor Street West and Parkside Drive ☎ 416/392-1111 🕐 Daily dawn to dusk 🍴 Snack bars 🚇 High Park ♿ Good 🎟 Free

The ravines

There are 21 of these parks in Toronto. Wooded and cut with streams, they shelter abundant natural life and offer great opportunities for birdwatching. At the Glen Stewart Ravine, which runs from Kingston Road and Glen Manor Road south toward Queen Street East, you can stroll the nature trail and see cardinals, chickadees, indigo buntings, and many other species.

KORTWRIGHT CENTRE FOR CONSERVATION

In 400 acres of the Humber River Valley: ll miles of trails, with guided walks, exhibits, and videos.

➕ Off map to northwest ✉ In Vaughan ☎ 416/661-6600 🕐 Daily 10–4 🍴 Café ♿ Good 🎟 Free

QUEEN'S PARK

The park extends in front and behind the provincial buildings. The area closest to the buildings is studded with statues of local heroes.

➕ J6 ✉ College and Avenue Road 🕐 Daily 🚇 Queen's Park ♿ Good 🎟 Free

TOMMY THOMPSON PARK

On an artificial peninsula extending into Lake Ontario, this park provides a nesting habitat for 29 bird species. Interpretive programs are offered on weekends and holidays in summer.

➕ Off map to southeast ✉ At end of Leslie Street on waterfront ☎ 416/661-6600 🕐 Sat, Sun, holidays 9–6 🚇 Leslie and Commissioners Streets, then free shuttle ♿ Few 🎟 Free

ATTRACTIONS FOR CHILDREN

AFRICAN LION SAFARI
Young visitors can sight lions, tigers, and other game in this 500-acre wildlife park, ride the *African Queen* or the scenic railway, and see animal performances. There are playgrounds too.
➕ Off map to southwest ✉ R R No. 1, Cambridge, ON. Take Highway 401 to Highway 6 south ☎ 519/623-2620 ⏱ Summer: daily 10–5:30. Spring/autumn: Mon–Fri 10–4; Sat–Sun 10–5. Closed Nov–Apr 🍴 Cafeteria/snack bar 💲 Very expensive

PLAYDIUM
A good selection of interactive games and simulators, rock-climbing walls, karting track, batting cages, IMAX theater.
➕ Off map to west ✉ 99 Rathburn Road West, Mississauga ☎ 905/273-9000 ⏱ Sun–Thu 10–midnight; Fri 10AM–4AM; Sat 10AM–2AM 🍴 Restaurant, café 🚇 Islington then bus No 20 ♿ Good 💲 Prices vary

RIVERDALE FARM
Early 20th-century farm by the Don Valley ravine.
➕ L7–M7 ✉ 201 Winchester Street ☎ 416/392-6794 ⏱ Daily 9–5 🚋 Carlton streetcar 💲 Free

WILDWATER KINGDOM
A huge water theme park with a wave pool, slides, giant hot tubs—and the Cyclone water ride.
➕ Off map to northwest ✉ Finch Avenue, 1 mile west of Highway 427, Brampton, ON ☎ 416/369-0123 or 905/794-0565 ⏱ May–mid-Jun: Sat–Sun 10–6. Mid-Jun–Labour Day: daily 10AM–11PM (water rides until 8) 🍴 Three restaurants ♿ Few 💲 Very expensive

YOUNG PEOPLE'S THEATRE
Presents adaptations of Charles Dickens, C. S. Lewis, and other authors' stories from October to May.
➕ K8–K9 ✉ 165 Front Street East, at Sherbourne Street ☎ Box office 416/862-2222. Administration 363-5131 🚇 Union, King ♿ Good 💲 Prices vary

That's entertainment
The city offers an astonishing array of children's entertainment. Many take place at Harbourfront, like the Saturday afternoon Cushion Concerts (for 5- to 12-year-olds), creative crafts on Sundays, daycamps during school breaks, plus the seven-day Milk International Festival of music, dance, theater, and puppetry in May.

Taking the weight of the world on his shoulders

57

GALLERIES

See Top 25 Sights for
HARBOURFRONT (► 42)
UNIVERSITY OF TORONTO (► 33)

BAU-XI

Paintings, sculpture, drawings, and prints by such contemporary Canadian artists as Jack Shadbolt and Hugh Mackenzie.

➕ H8 ✉ 80 Spadina Avenue at King Street ☎ 416/977-0600 🕐 Tue–Sat 10–5:30 🚋 King streetcar to Spadina 🎫 Free

BAY OF SPIRITS GALLERY

Totem poles, masks, prints, and jewelry by the Native Indians of the Pacific Coast.

➕ J9 ✉ 156 Front Street West ☎ 416/971-5190 🕐 Mon–Fri 10–6; Sat–Sun 11–5 🚋 Front streetcar 🎫 Free

Mask, Bay of Spirits Gallery

Inuit art specialists

Eskimo Art Gallery (➕ J9 ✉ 12 Queen's Quay West ☎ 416/366-3000) has high-quality Inuit sculptures with prices starting as low as $40. Isaacs/Inuit Gallery (➕ H6–J6 ✉ 9 Prince Arthur Avenue ☎ 416/921-9985) is a leading specialist in Arctic art and early Native Canadian art and artifacts. Feheley Fine Arts (➕ J5 ✉ 14 Hazelton Avenue ☎ 416/323-1373) has exhibited and sold Inuit art for more than 30 years.

GALLERY ONE

After more than twenty years on the city art scene, the gallery represents a raft of Canadian artists (e.g. Jack Bush, Kenneth Lockhead) and Americans (e.g. Helen Frankenthaler, Kenneth Noland, Stanley Boxer).

➕ J6 ✉ 121 Scollard Street ☎ 416/929-3103 🕐 Tue–Sat 10:30–5 🚋 Bay 🎫 Free

JANE CORKIN

A major photographic gallery that deals in both historical and contemporary photographs.

➕ J8 ✉ 179 John Street ☎ 416/979-1980 🕐 Tue–Fri 9:30–5:30; Sat 10–5 🚋 Osgoode 🎫 Free

MIRA GODARD

A major gallery representing such names as Botero, Robert Motherwell, Frank Stella, Larry Rivers, David Hockney, Jasper Johns, and Lawren Harris.

➕ J6 ✉ 22 Hazelton Avenue ☎ 416/964-8197 🕐 Tue–Sat 10–5 🚋 Bay 🎫 Free

MOOSE FACTORY GALLERY

Charles Pachter is one of Canada's leading contemporary artists. His portrait of Queen Elizabeth on a moose is an icon of Canadian pop art. This exhibit has new paintings, sculpture, books and cards.

➕ H8 ✉ 22 Grange Avenue ☎ 416/596-8452 for appointment 🚋 Osgoode 🎫 Free

NANCY POOLE'S STUDIO

Another veteran on the art scene representing a roster of 25 or so contemporary artists. Mounts fine single artist shows. Group shows often in summer.

➕ J6 ✉ 16 Hazelton Avenue ☎ 416/964-9050 🕐 Tue–Sat 10–5 🚋 Bay 🎫 Free

PUBLIC & OUTDOOR ART

See also Top 25 Sights for
CITY HALL (► 43)

GUILD INN
Historic architectural fragments dot the grounds of
the Guild Inn, including a white marble facade from
the Imperial Bank of Canada building. Enjoy brunch
or cocktails on the veranda and stroll through the
grounds to the Scarborough Bluffs.
➕ Off map to northeast ✉ 201 Guildwood Parkway, Scarborough
☎ 416/261-3331 🚇 Kennedy 💵 Free

CITY HALL
Many of the works that once graced Metro Hall have
been moved into City Hall and can be seen scattered
throughout the building.
➕ J8 ✉ Queen Street West ☎ 416/338-0338
🚇 Queen/Osgoode 💵 Free

MURAL ON THE "FLAT IRON" BUILDING
Approach the Gooderham or "flat iron" building
(1892) from the west and you are faced with a strange
mural by Derek Besant, installed in 1980. You can
make of it what you will.
➕ K9 ✉ 49 Wellington Street East at Church 🚇 Union
💵 Free

PASTURE
Tucked away in a courtyard by the
Aetna Centre, several stolid cows by
Joe Fafard sit in a pasture, a reminder
that Toronto's wealth was originally
derived from farming.
➕ J9 ✉ Aetna Centre/TDC 🚇 King 💵 Free

PRINCESS OF WALES THEATRE
The interior murals and other elements
designed by Frank Stella are stunning
for those who pay money to attend a
performance at this state-of-the-art
theater. But the exterior back wall's
explosion of color and abstraction is
free to all.
➕ J8 ✉ 300 King Street West 🚇 St. Andrew
💵 Free

THREE WAY PIECE NUMBER TWO
In front of city hall stands an abstract
form by Henry Moore. Known more
commonly as *The Archer*, it suggests
both solidity and flexibility.
➕ J8 ✉ Nathan Phillips Square 🚇 Osgoode
💵 Free

SkyDome's gargoyles
The figures leaning out from the
SkyDome (► 35) like modern
gargoyles were fashioned by
Michael Snow, who also created
the flock of geese in the Eaton
Centre. The 15 figures, all in
different postures of elation or
despair, make up *The Audience*.
They have been coated with
weather-resistant fiberglass and
covered with a bronze-like
metallic paint.

*Gooderham building's
intriguing west facade*

59

FREE ENTERTAINMENTS

See Top 25 Sights for
CITY HALL (➤ 43)
ONTARIO PARLIAMENT BUILDINGS (➤ 41)

All free

Gardens, parks, markets, churches, political debates, industrial tours, and cemeteries are free. So are some walking tours, like those at the university or those led by the Toronto Historical Board. Also free in summer, swimming at a municipal pool, and the theater in High Park. Visit the Royal Ontario Museum on Tuesday evening when you can donate whatever you like.

CBC BUILDING

In the grand atrium you can see radio hosts speaking into microphones and technicians keeping everyone on track. The little museum is fun and free. Enjoy a variety of clips from radio and TV, and take the free tour to see studios and sets, maybe cruising the racks of the awesome costume department, where everything is organized by period or decade.

➕ J9 ✉ 250 Front Street West ☎ 416/205-8605 ⏰ Tour times vary 🍴 Cafeteria 🚇 Union ♿ Good

CHUM/CITYTV

This is as far from CBC as you can possibly get. Toronto's radical media company doesn't have fixed studios: cameras roll wherever they are needed—on the roof, in the hallways, even outside. Extreme haircuts or pierced body parts are far from shocking; knowing what's hip is what matters. This is the station where you can air your gripes and have them put out on prime time if they're colorful enough. Despite the "anything goes" attitude, reservations are necessary for the very popular free tours, which are often filled six months in advance.

➕ J8 ✉ 299 Queen Street West ☎ 416/591-5757 ⏰ Tour times vary 🚇 Osgoode

TORONTO STOCK EXCHANGE

All trading is now electronic. The building houses a museum with interactive displays about stocks and finances, and the Design Exchange, promoting the newest and best Canadian design.

➕ J8 ✉ Exchange Tower, 2 First Canadian Place at King and York Streets ☎ 416/947-4670 ⏰ Call for tour times 🚇 King

WALKING THE NEIGHBORHOODS

Some of the best free entertainment is out on the streets. Chinatown (➤ 50) is colorful and there is plenty to look at in Queen Street West (➤ 51). For natural beauty, stroll around the Harbourfront (➤ 42) or visit the Beaches (➤ 50). A trip to the Toronto Islands (➤ 45), though not free, costs very little and takes you to another world—water, peace, and quiet.

Crowds on Dundas Street West

STREETCAR RIDING

It costs only $2 to ride a streetcar, and you are assured of some great visual entertainment. Among the best lines to ride are Queen Street, College, and Dundas.

TORONTO
where to...

NEIGHBORHOOD FAVORITES

Prices

Expect to pay per person for a meal, excluding drink

$ up to $30

$$ up to $50

$$$ more than $50

More local favorites

Taro Grill (❖ H8 ✉ 492 Queen Street West ☎ 416/504-1320) is hip. Grappa (❖ H7 ✉ 797 College ☎ 416/535-3337) is rustic Italian. Messis (❖ H6 ✉ 97 Harbord ☎ 416/920-2186) offers contemporary Northern Italian cuisine. Herbs (✉ 3187 Yonge ☎ 416/322-0487) is bistro at its best. All are small and serve good, reasonably priced cuisine.

A few tips

Restaurant bills include a 7 percent goods and service tax (GST), and 8 percent provincial sales tax (PST) which together equal 15 percent tax. Always tip on the pre-tax total of the bill. Most restaurants are smoke free. Call first if this is important to you. Well-dressed casual is acceptable in most restaurants. Men might feel more comfortable wearing a jacket in the more upscale dining spots.

BISTRO TOURNESOL ($)

Classic fixed-price French bistro serving mouth-watering pâtés, steamed salmon, steak frîtes and creme brulée.
❖ H5 ✉ 406 Dupont Street ☎ 416/921-7766 ◷ Dinner only. Closed Mon ◉ Dupont

BROWNE'S BISTRO ($$)

The well-heeled Rosedale crowd drape their minks over the chairs while they consume hearty fare at modest prices.
❖ K4 ✉ 4 Woodlawn Avenue ☎ 416/924-8132 ◷ Lunch Mon–Fri, dinner daily ◉ Summerhill

CITIES BISTRO ($$)

Home to a hip and savvy crowd who know great value when they taste it—Asian-accented dishes such as black tiger shrimp and pineapple salsa.
❖ G8 ✉ 859 Queen Street West ☎ 416/504-3762 ◷ Lunch Tue–Fri; dinner daily ◉ Queen Street West streetcar

GILLES' BISTRO ($$)

Succulent roast duck, calves' liver and grapes, Cajun crabcakes, in a narrow bistro which is run as a labor of love.
❖ J6 ✉ 1315 Bay Street ☎ 416/923-1005 ◷ Lunch Wed–Fri; dinner Mon–Sat ◉ Bay

KITKAT ($$)

A theater district clientele of journalists and TV and film people eat honey-garlic backribs, pasta dishes, and lemon chicken amid cat memorabilia and old movie posters.
❖ H8 ✉ 297 King Street West

☎ 416/977-4461 ◷ Lunch Mon–Fri; dinner Mon–Sat ◉ St. Andrew

LA BODEGA ($$)

Romantic Gallic atmosphere and market-fresh daily specials. Game and fish dishes, veal Calvados, steak *au poivre.* Good prix fixe. Outdoor dining in summer.
❖ J7 ✉ 30 Baldwin Street ☎ 416/977-1287 ◷ Lunch Mon–Fri; dinner Mon–Sat ◉ St. Patrick ◉ Dundas streetcar

LE SELECT ($$)

Bistro fare at moderate prices. Typical dishes are *bavette aux échalotes* and duck confit. Patio with jazz playing in the background. Really international wine list.
❖ H8 ✉ 328 Queen Street West ☎ 416/596-6405 ◷ Mon–Thu 11:30AM–11:30PM; Fri–Sat 11:30AM–midnight; Sun noon–10:30 ◉ Queen Street West streetcar

MORTON'S OF CHICAGO ($$$)

A steakhouse that is a cut above. The menu features USDA prime beef—the best.
❖ J6 ✉ 4 Avenue Road ☎ 416/925-0648 ◷ Dinner daily ◉ Bay/Museum

TRATTORIA GIANCARLO ($$)

Small and intimate in Little Italy. People come for the perfectly grilled dishes and the superlative pastas and risottos.
❖ G7 ✉ 41–43 Clinton Street at College ☎ 416/533-9619 ◷ Dinner Mon–Sat 6–11 ◉ College Street streetcar

NOTED FOR CUISINE

AVALON ($$$)

Inspired cuisine by top young chef Christopher McDonald. Small, elegant, and comfortable. Simple, full-flavored food with favorites like herb-roasted chicken and rib steak with horseradish sauce.

✚ J8 ✉ 270 Adelaide Street West at John ☎ 416/979-9918 🕐 Lunch Wed–Fri; dinner Mon–Sat 🚇 Osgoode, St. Andrew

BOBA ($$$)

Innovative cuisine combining different ethnic flavors (rice paper wrapped chicken breast with rice wine vinegar sauce).

✚ J5 ✉ 90 Avenue Road ☎ 416/961-2622 🕐 Dinner Mon–Sat 🚇 Bay or St. George

CENTRO ($$$)

Contemporary French-Italian cuisine superbly prepared and presented.

✚ K1 ✉ 2472 Yonge Street ☎ 416/483-2211 🕐 Dinner Mon–Sat 🚇 Eglinton

MERCER STREET GRILL ($$$)

Enticing fare such as Thai jumbo shrimp and scallops with fresh mango roll and sour orange vinaigrette. Try chocolate sushi for dessert.

✚ H8 ✉ 36 Mercer Street ☎ 416/599-3399 🕐 Lunch Mon–Fri; dinner daily 🚇 King, St. Andrew

NORTH 44 ($$$)

Excels in melding a variety of international flavors—try the rack of lamb with pecan mustard crust and Zinfandel sauce. Dramatic art deco-style

room. Upstairs wine bar.

✚ K1 ✉ 2537 Yonge Street ☎ 416/487-4897 🕐 Dinner Mon–Sat 🚇 Eglinton 🚌 97X

SARKIS ($$$)

One of the city's greatest chefs, Greg Couillard, turns out richly flavored dishes redolent with Caribbean and Asian herbs and spices. Duck breast roasted in a reduction of pomegranate, tamarind, honey and star anise, prawns in coconut curry sauce, or orange beef, are just a few of the inventive possibilities.

✚ K8 ✉ 67 Richmond Street East ☎ 416/214-1337 🕐 Lunch Mon–Fri; dinner daily 🚇 Queen

SCARAMOUCHE ($$$)

This established restaurant is still gathering rave reviews. There's imaginative use of ingredients and flavors especially in the accompaniments (e.g. caramelized onions with sautéed artichoke hearts, eggplant, leek, and roasted peppers). Pasta bar menu too.

✚ J4 ✉ 1 Benvenuto Place (off Edmund Avenue, south of St. Clair) ☎ 416/961-8011 🕐 Dinner Mon–Sat 🚇 St. Clair

TRUFFLES ($$$)

Toronto's premier hotel dining room, and one of the best restaurants in North America. The cuisine is fresh, unusual and flavorful, the decor in simple but luxurious good taste.

✚ J6 ✉ Four Seasons Hotel, 21 Avenue Road ☎ 964-0411 🕐 Dinner Mon–Sat 🚇 Bay

More gourmet spots

One of the city's best known chefs, Jamie Kennedy, is currently cooking at the Royal Ontario Museum (➤ 39), providing exquisitely fresh luncheon fare. The most legendary dining is found outside town at Eigensinn Farm (☎ 519/922-3128), where genius chef Michael Stadtländer presents four-hour-long dinners.

Other food favorites include:

Ore ✉ 45 Elm Street ☎ 416/597-0155

Winston's ✉ 104 Adelaide Street West ☎ 416/360-8888

Pangaea ✉ 1221 Bay Street ☎ 416/920-2333

Youki ✉ 4 Dundonald Street ☎ 416/924-2925

OUTDOOR PATIOS

Lakefront dining

For a lakefront seat, check out Harbourfront. In Queen's Quay, Spinnakers and the Boathouse Café both have outdoor terraces. At the eastern end of the harbor you can dine aboard a cruise ship at Captain John's (✚ K9 ☎ 416/363-6062), while farther west along the docks, Pier 4 (✚ J9 ☎ 416/203-5865) and Wallymagoo's Marine Bar (✚ J9 ☎ 416/203-6248), both attract lovers of fish and shellfish. Best of all, though, for a real-down-on-the-lakefront dining experience, bring your own picnic.

ALICE FAZOOLI'S ($$)
The patio is warmed by a fire and beautified by a fountain and gardenias, and often features live bands. Inside, the main draw is crabs and raw bar specialties; a wide range of wines by the glass.
✚ H8 ✉ 294 Adelaide Street West ☎ 416/979-1910 ⚫ Lunch and dinner daily ⚫ Osgoode, St. Andrew

BAMBOO ($)
The club-restaurant that launched reggae, salsa and other Caribbean/Latin American sounds in Toronto. The patio (fountains, murals, glass) has great appeal but the cuisine is undistinguished.
✚ H8 ✉ 312 Queen Street West ☎ 416/593-5771 ⚫ Lunch Wed–Sat; dinner daily ⚫ Osgoode

BIAGIO ($$)
One of the most entrancing patios in the city with splashing fountain and statuary—plus some of Toronto's best Italian cooking.
✚ K8 ✉ 157 King Street East ☎ 416/366-4040 ⚫ Lunch Mon–Fri; dinner Mon–Sat ⚫ King ⚫ King Street East streetcar

COURT HOUSE MARKET GRILLE AND CHAMBER LOUNGE ($$)
In this 1852 restored stone courthouse is a plain-language menu of grills and rotisseries. After, tour the hanging area and old jail cells with wax museum figures.
✚ K8 ✉ 57 Adelaide Street East ☎ 416/214-9379 ⚫ Lunch Mon–Fri; dinner daily ⚫ King

IL POSTO NUOVO ($$)
This place knows how to bring out the best in fresh fish, grilled or pan seared. Style in the homemade pasta and inventive ways with vegetables. Off-street patio in summer.
✚ J6 ✉ 148 Yorkville Avenue (in Hazelton Lanes) ☎ 416/968-0469 ⚫ Lunch and dinner Mon–Sat ⚫ Bay/Museum/St. George

JUMP CAFÉ/BAR ($$)
View of Commerce Court from the patio. Eclectic cuisine ranges from pizzas to chicken breast flavored with rosemary, honey, and balsamic vinegar.
✚ J8 ✉ 1 Wellington Street West ☎ 416/363-3400 ⚫ Lunch Mon–Fri; dinner Mon–Sat ⚫ King

MONSOON ($$)
A design award-winning restaurant. New Asia cuisine includes chargrilling, bamboo steaming and crisp frying.
✚ J8 ✉ 100 Simcoe Street ☎ 416/979-7172 ⚫ Lunch Mon–Fri; dinner Mon–Sat ⚫ St. Andrews

SOUTHERN ACCENT ($$)
In Markham Village, with a spacious canopy-covered brick patio. Gumbo, jambalaya, blackened fish, and other spicy dishes from Louisiana. Finish with bread pudding and bourbon sauce.
✚ G6 ✉ 595 Markham Street ☎ 416/536-3211 ⚫ Dinner daily; lunch summer only ⚫ Bathurst

TRADITIONAL CANADIAN

BLOOR STREET DINER ($)

Serving shoppers and late-nighters, it combines an espresso bar, a rotisserie where meats, poultry, and fish are prepared in Provençal style, and a *café-terrasse* (a great place to relax in summer).

✚ J6 ✉ 55 Bloor Street West in the Manulife Centre
☎ 416/928-3105 ⏰ Daily 7AM–1AM 🚇 Bay/Bloor-Yonge

CANOE ($$$)

On the 54th floor of the TDC building. Inventive cuisine making use of Canadian ingredients (Digby scallops, Alberta beef, Grandview venison).

✚ J8–9 ✉ 66 Wellington Street West ☎ 416/364-0054
⏰ Lunch and dinner Mon–Fri 🚇 Union

JOSO'S ($$)

The best place for fresh fish in Toronto. Select your own fish from the tray and it will be grilled, steamed, poached, or cooked in any way to please your palate. The calamari are legendary. Decor created by the owner, singer-entertainer Joseph Spralja.

✚ J5 ✉ 202 Davenport Road (just east of Avenue Road)
☎ 416/925-1903 ⏰ Lunch Mon–Fri; dinner Mon–Sat
🚇 Bay 🚌 Bus 6

MONTREAL ($$)

Serves such Quebecois favorites as pea soup and *tourtière* (a meat pie), plus terrific jazz next door.

✚ K8 ✉ 65 Sherbourne Street (at Adelaide) ☎ 416/363-0179
⏰ Lunch Mon–Fri; dinner Mon–Sat 🚇 Queen or King
🚋 Queen Street East streetcar

PANGAEA ($$$)

Tranquility and huge floral arrangements create an air of luxury here. Sophisticated cooking, with velvety soups and a French/Italian menu. A favorite with the entertainment biz. A delicious afternoon tea also available.

✚ J6 ✉ 1221 Bay Street
☎ 416/920-2323 ⏰ Lunch and dinner Mon–Sat 🚇 Bay

RODNEY'S OYSTER HOUSE ($$)

As close as you'll get to a Nova Scotia seafood shack, with steamed delicacies.

✚ K8 ✉ 209 Adelaide Street East ☎ 416/363-8105
⏰ Lunch and dinner Mon–Sat 🚇 King

SHOPSY'S ($)

One of the few delis left in Toronto, and the place to come for a thick pastrami or good corned beef sandwich.

✚ K9 ✉ 33 Yonge Street
☎ 416/365-3333
⏰ Mon–Wed 7AM–11PM; Thu–Fri 7AM–midnight; Sat 8AM–midnight; Sun 8AM–11PM
🚇 Union

YOUKI ($$)

A charming casual bistro with a menu of 38 small dishes that span north and southeast Asia with no cross-cultural borrowing. Plenty of zest in the dishes, but no ear-popping fire if you insist. The grills, barbecues, and spring rolls are good value, and desserts are a must.

✚ K6 ✉ 4 Dundonald Street
☎ 416/924-2925 ⏰ Dinner daily 🚇 Wellesley

Local Ontario wines

Ever since the VQA (Vintners' Quality Alliance) appellation was introduced in 1988, Ontario's wines have improved immensely, and now you will find them on the very best wine lists. Look for Cave Spring, Konzelmann, Stoney Ridge, and the big names—Inniskillin, Château des Charmes and Hillebrand. Canada's ice wine is internationally known. Made from grapes which have frozen on the vine, it is thick, rich, and sweet—delicious with *biscotti*.

DECKED OUT IN STYLE

Movenpick: no expense spared

It took $6.5 million to create Movenpick's Palavrion (✉ 270 Front Street West ☎ 416/979-0060), a two-story stage set featuring hand painted tiles on the floors and walls, extravagant lighting fixtures, and *trompe l'oeil* art. Eye-catching displays of fruits, vegetables, pastries, and other foodstuffs decorate Movenpick's Marché in the BCE Galleria (☎ 416/366-8986), where customers eat at tables set under artificial trees.

ACQUA ($$$)

Starfish pattern the floors, water cascades down a wall encrusted with metal fish, and striped poles demarcate the courtyard dining area. Contemporary Italian cuisine (grilled swordfish with Sicilian *pepperonata* and lemon, thyme and caper butter). Great selection of dessert wines, ports, and grappas.
✚ J9 ✉ 10 Front Street West ☎ 416/368-7171 🕐 Lunch Mon–Fri; dinner Mon–Sat 🚇 Union

AUBERGE DU POMMIER ($$$)

A French country-style *auberge* with the gardens, stone and architecture creating a romantic atmosphere. The food tends to be fussy, though.
✚ Off map to north ✉ 4150 Yonge Street at York Mills ☎ 416/222-2220 🕐 Lunch Mon–Fri; dinner Mon–Sat 🚇 York Mills

BISTRO 990 ($$$)

Informality and a superior kitchen combine to make this one of the hottest tickets in town for locals and stars working in "Hollywood North." A friendly welcome, attentive service and a menu featuring Provençal cuisine favorites explains why.
✚ J6 ✉ 990 Bay Street ☎ 416/921-9990 🕐 Lunch and dinner daily 🚇 Bay

GRANO ($$)

A riotous celebration of rustic Italy. Tables are painted in brilliant mustard and cherry red, wine is served in tumblers, and arias fill the air. The counter displays more than 50 antipasti. Pasta, meat, and fish dishes change daily. Casual and fun.
✚ K2 ✉ 2035 Yonge Street ☎ 416/440-1986 🕐 Mon–Fri 10AM–10:30PM; Sat 10AM–11PM 🚇 Davisville

THE MARCHÉ ($)

A vast indoor European market with the world's foods made to order before your very eyes at cooking stations. In-house bakery. Fill up your tray and dine in any one of seven themed seating areas.
✚ J9 ✉ 42 Yonge Street (in BCE Place) ☎ 416/366-8986 🕐 Breakfast, lunch and dinner daily 🚇 Union

MYTH ($$)

Giant shields adorn the walls and banks of TVs play movies based on Greek myths. Hot and cold appetizers plus pizza and pasta.
✚ N6 ✉ 417 Danforth Avenue ☎ 416/461-8383 🕐 Thu–Sat 11:30AM–4AM; Sun–Wed 11:30AM–2AM; lunch only Fri–Sat in winter 🚇 Chester

SPLENDIDO ($$)

A riot of brilliant yellow lit by a host of tiny lights, with huge canvases of sunflowers by Helen Lucas. Internationally inspired cuisine (pastas, pizzas, roast rack of veal in sun dried tomato *aioli*) lures crowds to this noisy, energized dining room.
✚ H6 ✉ 88 Harbord Street ☎ 416/929-7788 🕐 Dinner Mon–Sat 🚇 Spadina

COFFEE, CAKES & LIGHT BITES

BAR ITALIA ($)

Italian chic with an upstairs pool hall, and a downstairs café jammed at night with a young crowd.

📍 G7 ✉ 582 College Street
☎ 416/535-3621
🕐 Mon–Thu 11:30AM–11:30PM;
Fri 11:30AM–12:30AM; Sat 9:30AM
–12:30AM; Sun 9:30AM–11:30PM
🚊 College Street streetcar

BREGMAN'S BAKERY RESTAURANT ($)

Irresistible bagels, cakes, cookies and muffins. Full deli dining room upstairs with salads, big sandwiches, pasta and stirfrys.

📍 K4 ✉ 1560 Yonge Street
☎ 416/967-2750
🕐 Breakfast, lunch and dinner daily 🚊 St. Clair

CAFÉ DIPLOMATICO ($)

Still not gussied up, it has mosaic marble floors, wrought iron chairs, and a glorious cappuccino machine. A Toronto tradition on weekends.

📍 G7 ✉ 594 College Street
☎ 416/534-4637
🕐 Sun–Thu 8AM–1AM; Fri, Sat
8AM–2AM 🚊 College Street streetcar

CAFFÉ DEMETRE ($)

Crowd in for Belgian waffles and huge sundaes, cakes and baklava.

📍 N6 ✉ 400 Danforth Avenue ☎ 416/778-6654
🕐 Sun–Thu 1PM–1AM; Fri–Sat noon–3AM 🚊 Chester

DAILY EXPRESS CAFÉ ($)

An Annex community spot frequented by artists, students, and academics.

📍 H6 ✉ 280 Bloor Street
West ☎ 416/944-3225
🕐 Mon–Fri 7:30AM–midnight;
Sat–Sun 9–7 🚊 St. George

DUFFLET PASTRIES ($)

More than 100 appetizing tarts and pastries. Funky.

📍 H8 ✉ 787 Queen Street
West ☎ 416/504-2870
🕐 Mon–Sat 10–7; Sun noon–6
🚊 Queen Street West streetcar

EPICURE CAFÉ ($)

More than just a café—also full lunches or dinners. Hang out at the marble tables listening to the background jazz.

📍 H8 ✉ 512 Queen Street
West ☎ 416/504-8942
🕐 Mon–Thu 12PM–10PM; Fri, Sun
noon–11PM; Sat noon–midnight
🚊 Queen Street West streetcar

LAVA ($)

Vintage 60s decor with 90s food. Sushi, vegan fare, fragrant curries, sticky rice and wok-seared vegetables feature.

📍 G7 ✉ 507 College Street
☎ 416/966-5282 🕐 Lunch
and dinner daily 🚊 College,
then College streetcar westbound

SICILIAN ICE CREAM COMPANY ($)

Every Torontonian, it seems, swears this is the best ice cream in the city.

📍 G7 ✉ 710–712 College
Street ☎ 416/531-7716
🕐 Mon–Fri 9:30AM–midnight;
Sat 9–midnight; Sun
11–midnight 🚊 College Street
streetcar

SOTTOVOCCE ($)

Ritzy Milan-style coffee bar attracting an older, more sophisticated crowd.

📍 G7 ✉ 595 College Street
☎ 416/536-4564
🕐 Mon–Sat noon–1AM
🚊 College Street streetcar

Go home, Starbucks!

Now that the grounds have settled and the battle of the beans has stabilized into a cold war fought with iced Moccaccino, can you just get a regular cup of coffee anywhere? American-owned Starbucks goes head to head with locally owned Second Cup, and not too far behind it Timothy's World News Café. Lettieri is also a small chain with legions of fans. Second Cup is alive and inviting, with murals and individual ambience, and Timothy's offers plenty of reading material. To compete, Starbucks is launching its own magazine, *Joe*.

ETHNIC EXCELLENCE

Tables with a view

The 54th floor of Mies van der Rohe's TDC, Canoe (▶ 65) offers a view of surrounding skyscrapers. At the top of the Park Plaza, the Roof Restaurant (✉ 4 Avenue Road ☎ 416/924-5471) and the adjacent lounge afford great views of downtown. Scaramouche (▶ 63) offers window seats on the downtown skyline. The most stunning view of all is from 360 on top of the CN Tower (☎ 416/362-5411).

MIDDLE EASTERN/MEDITERRANEAN

BOUJADI ($)
Brightly colored family-run café hung with rugs, brass and pottery. No dairy products. Try *tagines*, *pastilla*, and *merguez* sausage. Honey pastries, mint tea and dance entertainment on Saturdays.
✚ K2 ✉ 220 Eglinton Avenue East ☎ 416/440-0258 🕔 Dinner Tue–Sat 🚇 Eglinton

CHIADO ($$)
Reminiscent of a Lisbon bistro. Stick to such signature Portuguese dishes as the marinated sardines, poached salted cod, and the *nato do céu*.
✚ F7 ✉ 864 College Street (at Concord Avenue) ☎ 416/538-1910 🕔 Lunch and dinner Mon–Sat 🚋 College Street streetcar

LA FENICE ($$)
The business crowd's favorite. Around 20 pasta dishes, plus fine Provimi veal and other delicious Italian fare.
✚ H8 ✉ 319 King Street West ☎ 416/585-2377 🕔 Lunch Mon–Fri; dinner Mon–Sat 🚇 St. Andrew

OUZERI ($$)
Very Athens. Spirited, casual, and crowded at night and on weekends. Exhaustive menu of appetizers and small plates of octopus, sardines with mustard, calamari, shrimp with feta and wine, plus traditional Greek dishes. Outdoor patio.
✚ N6 ✉ 500A Danforth Avenue ☎ 416/778-0500 🕔 Sun, Mon, Wed, Thu 11AM–11PM; Tue, Fri, Sat 11AM–2AM 🚇 Danforth

PAN ON THE DANFORTH ($$)
Among the kabob houses, this is one place where you find authentic exciting, updated Greek food. Some 20 appetizers head the menu, followed by such memorable dishes as loin of lamb with a fig and orange glaze. Contemporary Greek music.
✚ N6 ✉ 516 Danforth Avenue ☎ 416/466-8158 🕔 Dinner daily 🚇 Pape

ASIAN

EMA-TEI ($$)
Frequented by many Japanese because it delivers absolutely authentic cuisine, from the perfect appetizers to the fresh sushi.
✚ J8 ✉ 30 St. Patrick Street ☎ 416/340-0472 🕔 Lunch Mon–Fri; dinner daily 🚇 Osgoode

INTERNATIONAL ($)
This is the place to come for dim sum. On weekends, the vast room is filled with Chinese families and friends. Select from the dim sum carts, and enjoy a very moderately priced feast.
✚ H8 ✉ 421 Dundas Street West ☎ 416/593-0291 🕔 Lunch and dinner daily 🚋 Dundas Street streetcar

LAI WAH HEEN ($$$)
A beautiful meeting place. The excellent food is prepared in a specially equipped Cantonese

kitchen. Try the shark's fin soup, abalone or other extravagant dishes. Dim sum menu too.

➕ J8 ✉ 110 Chestnut Street in the Metropolitan Hotel ☎ 416/977-9899 🕐 Lunch and dinner daily Ⓢ Dundas/St. Patrick

LEE GARDEN ($)

A venerable Chinatown favorite still serving some of the best Chinese seafood dishes going— crab cooked with green onion and ginger, shrimp with pepper and eggplant plus oysters, clams, and abalone. There's traditional chicken, beef, and pork too, but it is the fish that you come for.

➕ H7 ✉ 331 Spadina Avenue ☎ 416/593-9524 🕐 Dinner daily from 4PM 🚋 Dundas streetcar or bus 77X

MATA HARI ($)

Coconut-scented curries, really fresh fish enhanced by sauces spiced with lime leaf, chilis, and red onion, spring rolls and satays all served in a halogen-lit setting.

➕ J7 ✉ 39 Baldwin Street (off Spadina) ☎ 416/596-2832 🕐 Lunch Tue–Fri; dinner Tue–Sun Ⓢ St. Patrick

NAMI ($$$)

Ultra-stylish and *very* expensive, this is frequented by Japanese business people and their guests. Prime attractions are the really fresh sushi and sashimi and darkly sophisticated decor.

➕ K8 ✉ 55 Adelaide Street East ☎ 416/362-7373 🕐 Lunch Mon–Fri; dinner Mon–Sat Ⓢ Queen or King

TIGER LILY'S ($)

Down-to-earth and very reasonably priced noodle house. At lunch it's cafeteria style, at dinner there's table service. Vietnamese-style sweet-and-sour rice noodles served with the fish of the day is just one great choice.

➕ J8 ✉ 257 Queen Street West ☎ 416/977-5499 🕐 Lunch and dinner daily Ⓢ Osgoode 🚋 Queen Street West streetcar

VANIPHA ($)

A hole-in-the-wall serving some of the best Laotian and Thai cuisine, from pad Thai to grilled fish with tamarind sauce. Sticky-rice lovers should try the version here.

➕ H7 ✉ 193 Augusta Avenue ☎ 416/340-0491 🕐 Lunch and dinner Mon–Sat 🚋 College Street streetcar

LATIN AMERICAN

XANGO ($$)

Authentic Latin American cuisine. *Ceviches* (raw fish with chopped onion and lime juice) to begin, and dishes from Central America, Ecuador, and Peru to follow—Peruvian *chupe* and *vaca frita* (steak in a herb and spice marinade) from Argentina for example, with plantain and *boniato* (sweet potato). Tile floors, wrought iron chairs, and intimate lighting. Interesting South American and Spanish wine list.

➕ J8 ✉ 106 John Street ☎ 416/593-4407 🕐 Dinner Mon–Sat (Thu–Sat in winter) Ⓢ St. Andrew

SHOPPING AREAS & DEPARTMENT STORES

Timothy Eaton

Timothy Eaton emigrated from Ireland in 1854 and set up shop in St. Mary's, Ontario. He arrived in Toronto in 1869 and opened a store on Yonge Street, where he started innovative merchandizing and marketing techniques, like fixed prices, cash-only sales, refunds, and mail order—all unique then. Sadly, many stores have since closed.

THE BAY

Good designer boutiques and a pleasant store to shop in. Take a break at SRO art deco bar restaurant.

✚ J8 ✉ 176 Yonge at Queen ☎ 416/861-9111 🚇 Queen

BLOOR STREET

The Canadian flagship store Holt Renfrew is here, along with haute retail—Chanel, Tiffany, Hermès, Lalique, Roots, and Gap, Body Shop, and Benetton.

✚ J6–K6 🚇 Bloor-Yonge

COLLEGE PARK & ATRIUM ON BAY

The first is a more intimate, less hectic version of Eaton Centre with 100 stores; the second is even smaller with 60 stores.

✚ J7 🚇 College ✚ J6 🚇 Bay

EATON CENTRE/ EATON'S

Anchored by the flagship eponymous department store, this huge mall contains over 350 stores over three levels. The perfume bar at Eaton's is alphabetically organized.

✚ J8–K8 ✉ Yonge between Dundas and Queen ☎ 416/598-2322 🚇 Dundas

HAZELTON LANES

This warren-like complex of over 85 stores has all the most prestigious names—Gianni Versace, Valentino, Fogal, Turnbull & Asser, Rodier, and Ralph Lauren. Lox, Stock and Bagel Deli opens to an appealing tree- and flower-filled courtyard for lunch in summer.

✚ J5–J6 🚇 Bay

HOLT RENFREW

Canada's answer to Harvey Nichols. Two floors of designer fashion, Daniel Galvin Salon, Estee Lauder Spa, perfumes and a café.

✚ J6 ✉ 50 Bloor Street West ☎ 416/922-2333 🚇 Bloor-Yonge

QUEEN STREET WEST

The hip shopping area where Canada's young designers rule. Fashions, antique clothing, flamboyant shoes, jewelry and household design.

✚ G8–J8 🚇 Osgoode

QUEEN'S QUAY

It's worth visiting this tourist shopping spot on the waterfront for the variety and quality of the stores— from Rainmakers, featuring whimsical umbrellas and insulated rainwear to Suitables, offering reasonably priced silk blouses.

✚ J9 🚊 LRT

ROOTS

The Canadian store *par excellence*. Started as a single store in 1973, Roots (➤ 76) is now an internationally recognized brand name. There are branches all over the city.

YORKVILLE

The premier shopping area. Yorkville and Cumberland Avenues are lined with boutiques selling everything from jewelry at Silverbridge and Peter Cullman, to leather at Lanzi of Italy and tobacco at Winston & Holmes. Many galleries and bookstores too.

✚ J6 🚇 Bloor-Yonge

ANTIQUES & COLLECTIBLES

C.C.LAI
Exquisite Asian antiques
fill this store—furniture
large and small, plus
porcelain, jade, jewelry,
and religious objects.
✚ J6 ✉ 9 Hazelton Avenue
☎ 416/928-0662 🚇 Bay

FIFTY ONE ANTIQUES
Specializes in 17th- and
18th-century furniture
(Empire, Biedermeier, and
other styles), along with
various decorative items:
vases, lamps, carvings,
European paintings, and
other accessories.
✚ J6 ✉ 21 Avenue Road
☎ 416/968-2416 🚇 Bay

**HARBOURFRONT
ANTIQUES MARKET**
(➤ 34)

MARK MCLAINE
A personal collection of
eclectic pieces—from
pine furnishings to
French sconces and
costume jewelry to
ceramics and sculpture.
Great browsing with prices
ranging from $20 to
thousands.
✚ J6 ✉ Hazelton Lanes
☎ 416/927-7972 🚇 Bay

MICHEL TASCHEREAU
There are wonderful
objects in this
idiosyncratic collection.
Huge armoires share space
with Canadian folk-art
objects, and a variety of
china, glass, and English
furniture.
✚ J6 ✉ 176 Cumberland
Street ☎ 416/923-3020
🚇 Bay

THE PAISLEY SHOP
Fine English furniture
specialist. Also carries

mirrors, porcelain, glass,
cushions, lamps, and
lighting fixtures.
✚ J6 ✉ 77 Yorkville Avenue
☎ 416/923-5830 🚇 Bay

R.A. O'NEILL
Country furniture from
around the world—
Germany, England,
Holland, and Ireland.
You'll find tables, chairs,
chests, and cupboards, as
well as such items as
decorative samplers or
decoys.
✚ J5 ✉ 100 Avenue Road
☎ 416/968-2806 🚇 Bay

**RED INDIAN AND
EMPIRE ANTIQUES**
An Alladin's cave full with
objects dating from the
1930s to 1950s. There's
everything you could
possibly imagine here—
neon signs, Bakelite
jewelry, lighting of all
sorts, Coca-Cola
memorabilia, and other
retro items.
✚ H8 ✉ 536 Queen Street
West ☎ 416/504-7706
🚋 Queen Street West streetcar

**SHOWCASE
ANTIQUE MALL**
Four floors containing
the wares of more than
300 dealers. You can
travel from art nouveau
to pop art, and from
coins and clocks to
jukeboxes, and Elvis
and Beatle memorabilia.
✚ H8 ✉ 610 Queen Street
West ☎ 416/703-6255
🚋 Queen Street streetcar

STANLEY WAGMAN
A major trader of period
French furniture.
✚ J5 ✉ 111 Avenue Road
☎ 416/964-1047 🚇 Bay

Tax refunds

Visitors can apply for a refund of
GST (goods and services tax) on
non-disposable items (➤ 90).
The easiest way to secure the
refund is to drop in at a duty-free
shop on the way out of Canada.
Fill out the forms, attach your
receipts and ask for the refund.
Or you can mail your claim. For
information contact Revenue
Canada (✚ J5 ✉ Summerside
Tax Centre, Summerside PE C1N
6C6 ☎ 902/432-5608).

CRAFTS & JEWELRY

Jewelry in the making

At 18 Karat (✚ J8 ✉ 71 McCaul Street in Village-by-the-Grange ☎ 416/593-1648), the craftspeople will copy any design that you wish. They will also repair or redesign antique settings. In Yorkville, shoppers can observe Peter Cullman fashioning beautiful pieces in his studio (✚ J5 ✉ 99 Yorkville Avenue in Cumberland Court ☎ 416/964-2196). Many items are inspired by natural and organic forms.

ALGONQUIANS SWEET GRASS GALLERY

Specializing in Native Canadian arts and crafts, the gallery is owned by an Ojibwa Indian and features Iroquois masks, porcupine quill boxes, Cowichan handknits from British Columbia, and much more.
✚ H8 ✉ 668 Queen Street West ☎ 416/703-1336
🚋 Queen Street West streetcar

BIRKS

A venerable Canadian name, selling jewelry, plus the best in china, crystal, silver, glass, and other table accessories.
✚ J6 ✉ Manulife Centre, 55 Bloor Street ☎ 416/922-2266
🚇 Bay

DU VERRE

Brilliant glass pieces catch the eye here at one of the favorite shops on the Toronto bride's wedding list.
✚ H8 ✉ 280 Queen Street West ☎ 416/593-0182
🚋 Queen Street West streetcar

FRIDA CRAFT STORES

An appealing store to browse through, with Canadian crafts alongside items from Asia, Africa, and Latin America. There are attractive fabrics, rugs, bags, costume jewelry, and candles, as well as a variety of knickknacks.
✚ K9 ✉ 39 Front Street East ☎ 416/366-3169 🚇 Union

GUILD SHOP

A prime place to purchase the latest and best in Canadian crafts including ceramics, glass, woodwork, jewelry, and textiles by named artists, as well as Inuit and Native Canadian art.
✚ J6 ✉ 118 Cumberland Street ☎ 416/921-1721
🚇 Bay

LYNN ROBINSON

Avant-garde design. Wonderful *raku* (Japanese-type glazed earthenware) and bronze pieces plus contemporary glass, clay, wood, and leather items made by Canadian craftspeople.
✚ G8 ✉ 709 Queen Street West ☎ 416/703-2467
🚋 Queen Street West streetcar

PRIME GALLERY

Inspiring and appealing ceramic and other crafted objects, terracotta, fabric and jewelry—ranging in price from reasonable to very expensive.
✚ J8 ✉ 52 McCaul Street ☎ 416/593-5750 🚇 Osgoode

SILVERBRIDGE

Marvelously sculptured pieces of sterling silver. Necklaces, bracelets, rings, and earrings for women, plus cuff links, money clips, and key holders for men, all beautifully crafted. Prices range from $60 to $1,600.
✚ J6 ✉ 162 Cumberland Street ☎ 416/923-2591
🚇 Bay

SNOW LION INTERIORS

Worth seeking out for its selection of Asian crafts. You'll also find Tibetan rugs, plus a variety of ceramics, fabrics, lamps, jewelry and more.
✚ K4 ✉ 575 Mount Pleasant Road ☎ 416/484-8859
🚇 St. Clair 🚋 Mount Pleasant

BOOKS

ABELARD

A book lover's dream, offering a broad and well-catalogued selection of antiquarian and second-hand books. Armchairs for browsing in comfort.

H8 519 Queen Street West 416/504-2665 Queen Street West streetcar

DAVID MIRVISH

Son of the famous Ed (► 8), David is an art lover and his store reflects his passion. It is filled with volumes on sculpture, painting, architecture, ceramics, photography, and other related subjects. Out-of-print and rare editions are also sold here.

G6 596 Markham Street 416/531-9975 Bathurst

LICHTMAN'S NEWS AND BOOKS

Friendly and casual with the newest books and a good selection of international newspapers and magazines.

K5 144 Yonge Street 416/368-7390 Bloor, St. Clair

NEW BALLENFORD

Interior design, graphic arts and architecture are the specialties in this store.

G6 600 Markham Street 416/588-0800 Bathurst

NICHOLAS HOARE BOOKSHOP

A store that invites browsing, especially for the latest British publications. Staff love books and can answer every question. There's a fireplace and comfy sofa.

K9 45 Front Street East 416/777-2665 Union

THE COOKBOOK STORE

Every conceivable book for the cook and lover of food and wine is arranged here according to cuisine from Afghan to Zimbabwean. There are also technical books for professional restaurateurs, as well as occasional special events.

K6 850 Yonge Street at Yorkville Avenue 416/920-2665 Bloor-Yonge

THEATREBOOKS

As the name suggests, this shop specializes in the performing arts. There are books and magazines on all aspects of theater, film, opera, and dance, including scripts and criticism.

J6 11 St. Thomas Street 416/922-7175 Bloor-Yonge

TORONTO WOMEN'S BOOKSTORE

This specialist bookstore carries all kinds of non-fiction titles on women's history, sexuality, and politics, as well as fiction of interest to women. It also stocks current magazines and journals relating to women's studies and at the same time functions as a community center.

H6 73 Harbord Street 416/922-8744 Spadina

ULYSSES

A well-stocked travel bookstore supplying maps, guidebooks and travel accessories.

J6 101 Yorkville Avenue between Bay and Avenue Road 416/323-3609 Bay

Major chains

According to World's Biggest Bookstore (J7–K7 20 Edward Street 416/977-7009), if you can't find a book in their store, then it doesn't exist. With 17 miles of shelves and more than a million books in this flagship store, that could be true. SmithBooks (J8–J9 Royal Bank Plaza 416/865-0090) is only one of this chain's many well-stocked general bookstores.

FASHIONS & RETRO

Canada's Own

Check out current Canadian fashion talent by visiting Eaton's and the Bay where they are grouped together. In the Bloor-Yorkville area you'll find Canada's best-known designer Alfred Sung; as well as Marilyn Brooks, a venerable mentor of the fashion scene; Nina Mdivani, for theatrical-style women's fashions; Vivian Shyu, for sophisticated but simple women's fashion; Lida Baday, for high-end fashion; Marisa Minicucci; and Dominic Bellissimo, the leather king. Native Torontonian Franco Mirabelli has his own Portfolio store in Eaton Centre. Queen Street West is the domain of young designers: John Fluevog (shoes), Angi Venni, Robin Kay (New Age environmentally correct interior design and fashions), and Kingi Carpenter (groovy, hip fashions).

BULLOCH TAILORS

This is where the city's professional, political, and military men traditionally come to be kitted out. Bespoke suits begin at $995.

K8 ✉ 43 Colborne Street ☎ 416/367-1084 Ⓜ Union

CABARET

Just the place to buy period costume and retro fashions. Seek out velvet and sequined gowns or that perfect smoking jacket.

H8 ✉ 672 Queen Street West (west of Palmerston) ☎ 416/504-7126 Ⓜ Osgoode Ⓣ Queen Street West streetcar

CHANEL

Classic high fashion from the famous French name. This is one of only two boutiques in Canada. It carries Chanel's full line, plus accessories.

J6 ✉ 131 Bloor Street ☎ 416/925-2577 Ⓜ Bay, Bloor-Yonge

CHEZ CATHERINE

Come here for designer fashions for women. A broad selection of creations by top designers, including Versace, Ferré, and Krizia.

J6 ✉ 55 Avenue Road ☎ 416/967-5666 Ⓜ Bay

F/X

Outrageous fashions, including those by British (eccentric) trendsetter Vivienne Westwood, fill the racks at this hip store. Also on Spadina and Yorkville.

H8 ✉ 515 Queen Street West ☎ 416/703-5595 Ⓣ Queen Street West streetcar

GEORGE BOURIDIS

Toronto's premier shirtmaker stocks more than 400 fabrics from all over the world. Custom-made shirts start at $135; a silk blouse will set you back at least $250.

K8 ✉ 193 Church Street between Dundas and Shuter Street ☎ 416/363 4868 Ⓜ Dundas

HARRY ROSEN

Three floors of fashions for men including all the top men's designers—Armani, Valentino, Calvin Klein, and Hugo Boss.

J6 ✉ 82 Bloor Street West ☎ 416/972-0556 Ⓜ Bloor-Yonge or Bay

MR MANN

Over the years Cy Mann has dressed many famous American and Canadian stars. His suits are meticulously crafted. A custom-made suit will take between four to six weeks to make.

J6 ✉ 41 Avenue Road ☎ 416/968-2022 Ⓜ Bay

MARILYN BROOKS

This is the store to find the current crop of Canadian fashion designers.

J6 ✉ 132 Cumberland Street ☎ 416/961-5050 Ⓜ Bay, Bloor-Yonge

STOLLERY'S

Long-established store with a distinct English flavor. Originally it catered for men only, but now has women's clothes, from the likes of Austin Reed and Burberry.

K6 ✉ 1 Bloor Street West ☎ 416/922-6173 Ⓜ Bloor-Yonge

FOOD & HOUSEHOLD GOODS

ALL THE BEST FINE FOOD

Best breads, salads, entrées, jams, relishes, sauces, and cheeses. Take a leaf out of the book of Rosedale's residents.
🕂 K5 ✉ 1099 Yonge Street ☎ 416/928-3330 🚇 Rosedale

ARLEQUIN

The mouthwatering display will tempt you to put together a gorgeous picnic feast of pâtés, salads, and pastries.
🕂 J5 ✉ 134 Avenue Road ☎ 416/928-9521 🚇 Bay, St. George

DANIEL ET DANIEL

All kinds of foods can be purchased here—from a cappuccino and croissant for breakfast to pâtés, mini-pizzas, quiches, salads, and hot and cold hors d'oeuvres for lunch.
🕂 K7 ✉ 246 Carlton Street ☎ 416/968-9275 🚇 College 🚊 Carlton streetcar

DINAH'S CUPBOARD

A charmingly cluttered and inviting store. There are plenty of dishes that can help make a picnic, along with mini-meals you can heat up in the microwave.
🕂 J6 ✉ 50 Cumberland Street ☎ 416/921-8112 🚇 Bloor-Yonge

EN PROVENCE

A beautiful store featuring household treasures from France—ceramics, table accessories, and luxurious fabrics. The tablecloths, napkins and china are fabulous.
🕂 J6 ✉ 20 Hazelton Avenue ☎ 416/975-9400 🚇 Bay

FORTUNE HOUSEWARES

This is the place to browse for top-of-the-line housewares that are sold at up to 20 percent off their normal price elsewehere. Brand-name cookware, plus utensils, and every kind of kitchen gadget.
🕂 H7 ✉ 388 Spadina Avenue ☎ 416/593-6999 🚇 Dundas or College streetcar, bus 77X

SEN5ES RETAIL AND BAKERY

This street-level shop features exquisite pastries, breads, terrines, smoked and cured salmon, caviar, overfilled sandwiches and caviar and blinis to take out.
🕂 J6 ✉ 15 Bloor Street West ☎ 416/935-0400 🚇 Bloor

TEN REN TEA

In the center of Chinatown, this store stocks fine teas in urns and also sells such items as slimming tea and health-oriented infusions. You will also find stocks of tiny, eminently collectible Chinese teapots and teacups.
🕂 H8 ✉ 454 Dundas Street West at Huron ☎ 416/598-7872 🚇 Dundas streetcar

TEUSCHER OF SWITZERLAND

This store offers an extraordinary range of chocolate—more than 100 different types in fact, including 20 or so truffles. They are handmade in Switzerland.
🕂 J6 ✉ 55 Avenue Road in Hazelton Lanes ☎ 416/961-1303 🚇 Bay, St. George

Picnic spots

Toronto has so much green space that finding a picnic spot is not a problem. The best locations are some of the most obvious—the Toronto Islands, the lakefront at Harbourfront or farther west at Sunnyside, the beach in the Beaches neighborhood, and High Park. Downtown, join the workers in Nathan Phillips Plaza or any of the grand spaces at the base of such towers as the TDC. Cumberland Park is an unusual city park featuring groves of indigenous trees, herbs, flowers and a mega-ton rock. It takes up a half of the block of Cumberland between Avenue Road and Belair.

FUN & LEISURE

For magazine maniacs

Great Canadian News Co. (➕ J9 ✉ BCE Place ☎ 416/363-2242), with its 2,000 magazines and 60 newspapers from around the world, is a magazine lover's paradise. Lichtman's News & Books (➕ K8 ✉ 144 Yonge Street ☎ 416/368-7390) helps to satisfy newshounds and also sells books. Maison de la Presse Internationale (➕ J6 ✉ 124 Yorkville Avenue ☎ 416/928-2328) stocks the widest selection of foreign publications.

CLUB MONACO

For casual, young fashions there is nowhere better than this chain, which has several stores in the city. This is the flagship store.
➕ H8 ✉ Corner of Queen's Park Circle and Bloor ☎ 416/979-5633 🚇 Queen Street West streetcar

JOHN FLUEVOG

The most flamboyant shoes you can imagine are found at this ultra-hip outlet. Madonna and Paula Abdul shop here.
➕ J8 ✉ 242 Queen Street West ☎ 416/581-1420 🚇 Queen Street West streetcar

KIDDING AWOUND

The collection of music boxes and clockwork toys will inspire adult nostalgia. Fun items from the 1950s to the '90s. If you can wind it, it's here.
➕ J9 ✉ 91 Cumberland Street ☎ 416/926-8996 🚇 Bay

OH YES, TORONTO

Yes, it deals in really bad-taste souvenirs that shout the city's name. They are mostly good quality and more attractive than what's on offer elsewhere.
➕ J6 ✉ 101 Yorkville Avenue ☎ 416/924-7198 🚇 Bay, Bloor-Yonge

PETER FOX

Women who have ever worn the shoes from this Vancouver designer love them for their fit and for their elegant and Victorian-romantic design. Satin or leather, they're quite exquisite.
➕ J6 ✉ 55 Bloor Street West ☎ 416/960-5572 🚇 Bloor-Yonge

ROOTS

Designs and sells fine-quality leather jackets, handbags, carrying cases, shoes and boots. Wool melton cloth and leather outerwear (such as the 2000 Olympics jackets worn by Prince Charles and Princes William and Harry) are renowned. There's also Roots for the home: upholstery, wooden furniture, bedding and a line of toiletries and jewelry.
➕ J6 ✉ 95 Bloor Street West ☎ 416/323-3289 🚇 Bay

TILLEY ENDURABLES

This store bears the name of the man who developed the "Tilley Hat," which can be used for a variety of purposes out in the wilderness. The store also stocks a range of other great outdoors gear, including a multi-pocketed jacket that is invaluable for traveling photographers.
➕ J9 ✉ 207 Queen's Quay West ☎ 416/203-0463 🚇 Union then LRT

WINSTON & HOLMES

Very English in style, it sells the accessories that men are supposed to need for their coiffure, their toilet, and their pleasure. There's a full range of pipes and pipe tobacco as well as cigars, including Cuban. There are even good old-fashioned fountain pens, and a professional barber offering a super deluxe shave.
➕ J6 ✉ 138 Cumberland Street ☎ 416/968-1290 🚇 Bay, Bloor-Yonge

GIFTS & MISCELLANEOUS

ASHLEY CHINA

It stocks all the great names not only in china but also in glass (Baccarat, Kosta Boda, Waterford). The goods are displayed elegantly in table settings or in wall cases.

✚ J6 ✉ 55 Bloor Street West ☎ 416/964-2900 🔇 Bloor-Yonge

DRAGON LADY COMIC SHOP

If you are looking for an unusual, reasonably priced gift, try here. It sells comics dating back to 1950, and also posters and back issues of *Life* magazine.

✚ G7 ✉ 609 College Street at University ☎ 416/536-7460 🔇 College

GENERAL STORE

This store stocks all kinds of attractively designed and personalized items—calculators, Swatch watches, Filofaxes, and no end of gadgets. Puzzles and brainteasers too.

✚ J6 ✉ 55 Avenue Road (Hazelton Lanes) ☎ 416/323-1527 🔇 Bay

THE GUILD SHOP

Fine Canadian crafts by Inuit, First Nations, and local artisans. A vast selection of soapstone carvings, jewelry, leather, glass, pottery, wood, and textiles.

✚ J6 ✉ 118 Cumberland Street ☎ 416/921-1721 🔇 Bay, Yonge

THE IRISH SHOP

A broad selection of gifts, fashions, and books from Ireland. You can pick up a kilt, a shawl, some lace, or an item of jewelry.

✚ J6 ✉ 150 Bloor Street West ☎ 416/922-9400 🔇 Bay, Bloor-Yonge

L'ATELIER GREGORIAN

This is a store for the devoted music lover. It contains a stunning collection of classical music and jazz CDs.

✚ J6 ✉ 70 Yorkville Avenue ☎ 416/922-6477 🔇 Bloor-Yonge

LEGENDS OF THE GAME

Sports fans head here to purchase the shirt, hat, or signed gear of their favorite team or player. Needless to say, it doesn't come cheap.

✚ J8 ✉ 322A King Street West ☎ 416/971-8848 🔇 St. Andrew

ROTMAN HAT

This old-established store offers a great range of hats—feather-light panamas, jaunty derbies, and so-called "grouser hats," as worn in the African jungle.

✚ H7 ✉ 345 Spadina Avenue ☎ 416/977-2806 🚋 Dundas or College streetcars, bus 77X

SCIENCE CITY

Here, you will find chemistry experiment kits, fossil specimens, hologram watches, and all kinds of science-oriented games and books. For the seriously scientific, there are also some expensive optical instruments, including telescopes.

✚ J6 ✉ 50 Bloor Street West in Holt Renfrew Centre ☎ 416/968-2627 🔇 Bloor-Yonge

Museum stores

The Art Gallery of Ontario store (➤ 37) offers reproductions, posters, jewelry, ceramics, glass, fabrics, and books. The Royal Ontario Museum's five stores (➤ 39) have similar lines, along with good replicas of museum pieces, including jewelry and toy soldiers. The George R. Gardiner Museum of Ceramic Art (➤ 40) has a fine selection of ceramic items, while the fabric selection at the Museum for Textiles (➤ 54) is truly exotic.

Music, Dance & Theater

Major venues

The city's major performing arts venues include:

Massey Hall

✚ K8 ✉ 178 Victoria Street
☎ 416/ 593-4828

Hummingbird Centre (formerly the O'Keefe Centre)

✚ K9 ✉ 1 Front Street East
☎ 416/ 872-2262

St. Lawrence Centre for the Arts

✚ K9 ✉ 27 Front Street East
☎ 416/366-7723

Roy Thomson Hall

✚ J8 ✉ 60 Simcoe Street
☎ 416/593-4828

Ford Centre for the Performing Arts

✉ 5040 Yonge Street ☎ 416/872-2222

Premiere Dance Theatre

✚ J9 ✉ Queen's Quay Terminal ☎ 416/973-4000

CLASSICAL MUSIC

CANADIAN OPERA COMPANY

The company was formed in 1950, and performs a season of six productions between September and April at the Hummingbird Centre.

✚ K9 ✉ 227 Front Street East
☎ 416/363-6671 or 872-2262
Ⓢ Union

TAFELMUSIK

This internationally known chamber group plays baroque music on authentic period instruments at Massey Hall or at Trinity/St. Paul's United Church at 427 Bloor Street.

✚ H6 ✉ 427 Bloor Street West ☎ 416/964-6337
Ⓢ Spadina

TORONTO MENDELSSOHN CHOIR

The choir was founded in 1895, when it gave its first performance at Massey Hall. It performs the great choral works of Bach, Handel, Elgar, and others as well as those of Mendelssohn. A claim to fame for the choir is that it sang Handel's *Messiah* for the soundtrack of the Spielberg film *Schindler's List*. It usually performs at Roy Thomson Hall.

✚ J8 ✉ 60 Simcoe Street
☎ 416/598-0422 or 593-4828
Ⓢ St. Andrew

TORONTO SYMPHONY ORCHESTRA

The symphony, which celebrates its 80th anniversary in 2001, performs a season at Roy Thomson Hall with top guest artists. In addition to its classical repertoire it performs light popular music and puts on a very well-supported regular series of outdoor summer concerts.

✚ J8 ✉ 60 Simcoe Street
☎ 416/593-4828 Ⓢ St. Andrew

DANCE

Except for the National Ballet, most companies perform at the Premiere Dance Theatre in Queen's Quay.

DANNY GROSSMAN DANCE COMPANY

Born in San Francisco, Danny Grossman became a local favorite when he began working with Toronto Dance Theatre in 1973, before founding his own company in 1975. Since then he has choreographed some 30 original works exhibiting social concern, wit, fun, and arresting physicality.

✚ H6 ✉ 425 Queen Street West ☎ 416/408-4543
Ⓢ Osgoode

NATIONAL BALLET OF CANADA

A beloved national icon. Founded by Celia Franca in 1951, the company has gained a golden international reputation for itself, with such stars as Karen Kain and Kimberly Glasco. It performs an autumn-to-spring season at the Hummingbird Centre that includes classics and modern pieces.

✚ K8 ✉ 470 Queen's Quay West ☎ 416/345-9686 or (tickets) 872-2262 Ⓢ LRT

TORONTO DANCE THEATRE

This is the leading contemporary dance company in Toronto. Directed by Christopher House, the company performs energetic choreographic works set to often surprising music. Examples are the Handel *Variations* and Artemis *Madrigals*. The company's performance venue is the Premiere Dance Theatre at Queen's Quay.

➕ L7 ✉ 80 Winchester Street ☎ 416/973-4000 🚋 Carlton streetcar

THEATER

BUDDIES IN BAD TIMES THEATRE

Not only is this the premier gay theater in Canada, it has also nurtured many contemporary straight writers. Its reputation was built by Sky Gilbert. On the cutting edge, it always delivers theater that challenges social boundaries. Additional draws are Tallulah's Cabaret (very popular Fri and Sat) and the bar.

➕ K7 ✉ 12 Alexander Street ☎ 416/975-8555 🚇 College, Wellesley

CANADIAN STAGE COMPANY

A company that produces comedy, drama, and musicals by international and Canadian authors. This is the company, for example, that brought the Broadway hit *Angels in America* to Toronto. Its home base is the St.

Lawrence Centre for the Arts, and it also puts on free summer performances in High Park.

➕ L8 ✉ 26 Berkeley Street ☎ 416/368-3110 🚋 King Street East streetcar

FACTORY THEATRE

Dedicated to producing the works of new Canadian playwrights which are put on in two theaters. Many of the company's productions have been on international tours and have had some success abroad.

➕ H8 ✉ 125 Bathurst ☎ 416/504-9971 or 864-9971 🚋 Bathurst streetcar

TARRAGON THEATRE

Another long-lasting Canadian theater company devoted to producing Canadian works by now-famous playwrights such as Michael Ondaatje, Michel Tremblay, and Judith Thompson. Off-Broadway productions sometimes arrive here too. Small and intimate.

➕ H4 ✉ 30 Bridgman Avenue ☎ 416/531-1827 🚇 Dupont

THEATRE PASSE MURAILLE

This is another company that nurtures contemporary Canadian playwrights. It produces innovative and provocative works by such figures as Daniel David Moses and Wajdi Mouawad. The theater has two stages, one catering for an audience of 220, the other for just 70.

➕ H8 ✉ 16 Ryerson Avenue ☎ 416/504-7529 🚋 Queen Street West streetcar or streetcar south from Bathurst

Landmark theaters

The grand Elgin and Winter Garden theaters (✉ 189–91 Yonge Street ☎ 416/872-5555) are built one on top of the other. The Royal Alexandra Theatre (✉ 260 King Street West ☎ 416/872-1212) is Toronto's beloved, 1907 baroque, red-and-gilt venue. Next door is the Princess of Wales Theatre (☎ 416/872-1212), built for *Miss Saigon* and decorated by Frank Stella.

COMEDY, DINNER THEATER & FILM

Exporting laughter

Canadians are thought of as a staid bunch, compared with their neighbors to the south. Yet much of what Americans laugh at is either written or performed by Canadians—from *Saturday Night Live* and *SCTV* to *Spy Magazine* to *The Kids in the Hall*. Lorne Michaels, Earl Pomerantz, Dan Aykroyd, Wayne and Shuster, John Candy, Martin Short, Jim Carrey, Howie Mandel… Canadians have a great talent for irony and satire.

COMEDY

THE LAUGH RESORT
Monique and other up-and-coming comedy performers appear at this very modestly priced venue.

✚ K8 ✉ 26 Lombard Street ☎ 416/364-5233 🚇 Queen

SECOND CITY
This venue is the source of so many Canadian comics who were to make it big in the U.S.—John Candy, Dan Aykroyd, Bill Murray, Martin Short, and others.

✚ H9 ✉ 56 Blue Jays Way ☎ 416/343-0011 🚇 Union

YUKYUK'S
The other home of great Canadian comedy. Begun in the 1960s and modeled on similar theaters in New York and Los Angeles, this venue nurtured such Canadian comedy stars as Jim Carrey, Harland Williams, Howie Mandel, and Norm MacDonald. It has also hosted American comics, some of the big names being Jerry Seinfeld, Robin Williams, and Sandra Bernhard.

✚ K2 ✉ 2335 Yonge Street ☎ 416/967-6425 🚇 Eglinton

DINNER THEATER

FAMOUS PEOPLE PLAYERS DINNER THEATRE
This group specializes in a unique form of theater called black light theater. Black-clad players move around manipulating lifesize puppets of famous people (Liberace, Barbra Streisand etc.) and props.

The bar was sponsored by the actor, Paul Newman and the theater by Elton John. The troupe has had great success on Broadway in New York.

✚ F8 ✉ 110 Sudbury Street ☎ 416/532-1137 🚇 Queen streetcar to Dovercourt

LA CAGE DINNER THEATRE
A campy concert given by female impersonators. Buddy Holly, Otis Redding, and Elvis are among the many who "appear" here.

✚ K8 ✉ 279 Yonge Street ☎ 416/364-5200 🚇 Dundas

LIMELIGHT SUPPER CLUB
Musical revues and other light entertainment are the staples of this club. There are dinner-and-show or show-only options.

✚ K2 ✉ 2026 Yonge Street ☎ 416/482-5200 🚇 Davisville (3 blocks north)

FILM

CARLTON CINEMAS
The place to see subtitled foreign films and cutting-edge North American independent films.

✚ K7 ✉ 20 Carlton Street ☎ 416/964-2463 🚇 College

CINÉMATHÈQUE ONTARIO
Organizes showings of directors' retrospectives, contemporary Canadian, and international films, and documentaries. All the films are screened at the Art Gallery of Ontario.

✚ K7 ✉ 2 Carlton Street ☎ 416/967-7371 🚇 College

ROCK, REGGAE, FOLK, JAZZ & BLUES

BAMBOO
The club that launched reggae and salsa in the city. Today it has calypso, salsa, hip, soul, and R&B in a Caribbean backdrop. Small dance floor.
➕ H8 ✉ 312 Queen Street West ☎ 416/593-5771
🔵 Osgoode 🚋 Queen Street West streetcar

EL MOCAMBO
The legendary rock place where the Stones performed. Suitably grungy, with local bands Monday nights and artists like Liz Phair on weekends.
➕ H7 ✉ 464 Spadina Avenue ☎ 416/968-2001 🚋 College streetcar

FREETIMES CAFÉ
Go to hear the folk acoustic entertainment. Mondays is open house, so bring your instrument and sign up at 7PM.
➕ H7 ✉ 320 College Street between Major and Roberts ☎ 416/967-1078 🚋 College streetcar

HORSESHOE TAVERN
A sawdust-on-the-floor-type place, where The Police, The Band, Blue Rodeo, and Barenaked Ladies got their start in Canada. Live rock-and-roll music Mon–Wed.
➕ H8 ✉ 370 Queen Street West ☎ 416/598-4753
🔵 Osgoode 🚋 Queen Street West streetcar

JUDY JAZZ
A sophisticated jazz-restaurant that hosts modern trios and groups six nights a week.
➕ H8 ✉ 370 King Street

☎ 416/593-7788
🔵 St. Andrew

LEE'S PALACE
Venue for the latest in rock music including up-and-coming Britpop groups. Home to local alternative bands. Dance bar with DJ.
➕ H6 ✉ 529 Bloor Street West ☎ 416/532-7383
🔵 Bathurst

MONTREAL JAZZ CLUB
Long-standing jazz venue hosting international and local talent such as Marion McPartland, Carol Welsman Quartet, and Memo Acevedo Quintet.
➕ K8 ✉ 65 Sherbourne Street ☎ 416/363-0179 🚋 King Street streetcar

PHOENIX CONCERT THEATRE
Patti Smith, Screaming Headless Torso, and Smashing Pumpkins have played here. Dance at weekends in an Egyptian-Greek fantasy set.
➕ K7 ✉ 10 Sherbourne Street ☎ 416/323-1251
🔵 Wellesley, College

RIVOLI
Hip club-restaurant for an eclectic mix of grunge, blues, rock, jazz, cabaret and poetry reading.
➕ H8 ✉ 332 Queen Street West ☎ 416/532-1598 or 596-1908 🔵 Osgoode 🚋 Queen Street West streetcar

TOP O' THE SENATOR
Relax on the couches or the old cinema seats in this 1930s jazz/cabaret spot.
➕ K8 ✉ 249 Victoria Street ☎ 416/364-7517 🔵 Dundas

Low-cost tickets & information
Get day-of-performance half-price tickets at the T.O. Tix booths at Yonge and Dundas Streets inside the Eaton Centre (➕ K8 🔵 Tue–Sat noon–7:30 ☎ 416/536-6468 ext 1).
To find out what's on try *Toronto Life*, *Where Toronto* and the weekend editions of the *Globe & Mail*, *Toronto Star*, and *Toronto Sun*. *Eye* or *Now* cover the hip scene, *Xtra!* the gay action.

DANCE CLUBS

Cyber, cigar, & pool scenes

Dotcom Café (✚ J8 ✉ 57 Duncan Street ☎ 416/595-5999) is the largest cyber café with 35 computers available for $10 an hour. Humidors have a major presence at Black and Blue (✚ J6 ✉ 150 Bloor Street ☎ 416/920-9900). Pool hustlers have endless choices including the purists' 24-hour Billiards Academy (✚ N6 ✉ 485 Danforth ☎ 416/486-9696).

Age limit

The legal drinking age in Ontario is 19, and young people should be prepared to show photo ID because entry and/or alcohol service can be refused.

BERLIN

Assorted sounds—Latin, hip-hop, top 40, R&B, and house—attract a more sophisticated crowd to this comfortable club.
✚ K2 ✉ 2335 Yonge Street
☎ 416/489-7777
🚇 Davisville

EL CONVENTO RICO

Famed for its weekend 1AM drag shows. Lambada the night away until 4AM.
✚ J7 ✉ 750 College Street
☎ 416/588-7800 🚋 College
🚋 College streetcar west

CHICK 'N' DELI

The dance floor gets jammed at this youthful TOP 40 R&B spot. Refuel with chicken wings and barbecue dishes.
✚ K2 ✉ 744 Mount Pleasant Road ☎ 416/489-3363
🚇 Eglinton

CROCODILE ROCK

Bar-restaurant and dance space that features slams on Saturday night. The 25- to 40-year-old crowd grooves to '70s and '80s dance sounds. Pool too.
✚ J8 ✉ 240 Adelaide Street West at Duncan ☎ 416/599-9751 🚇 St. Andrew

CUTTY'S HIDEAWAY

A mellow club on the Danforth where a Caribbean crowd sways to salsa and reggae. All ages.
✚ N6 ✉ 538 Danforth Avenue ☎ 416/463-5380
🚇 Chester

DELUGE AT ATLANTIS

Waterfront venue with house and high-energy dance music for the young crowd. Weekends only.
✚ F10 ✉ Ontario Place

EASY & THE FIFTH

An older crowd gathers in the loft-like space. The music leans more to the romantic and even allows for real conversation. Cigar bar with Oriental rugs and plush couches.
✚ H8 ✉ 225 Richmond Street West ☎ 416/979-3000
🚇 Osgoode

FLUID LOUNGE

Good-looking and hip dressers gain entry to the "underwater styled" venue to dance to the neo funk, industrial and other up-to-the-minute music. Check for celebrities.
✚ H8 ✉ 217 Richmond Street West ☎ 416/593-6116
🚇 Osgoode

INDUSTRY

Strobes and sound blasters maintain the pace. It really begins to throb at 2AM and goes on until dawn.
✚ G8 ✉ 901 King Street West ☎ 416/260-2660 🚋 King Street West streetcar

IVORY

Plush club for 30-plus including a number of models and their escorts. Saturday is most popular but Sunday is exotic Middle-Eastern night with Arabic music.
✚ J6 ✉ 69 Yorkville
☎ 416/927-9929 🚇 Bay

THE DOCKS

Super nightlife action in 41,000 square feet, with bar, dance club, restaurant, patio, indoor volleyball court, and paintball target range. For the young and beautiful on Lake Ontario.
✚ L10 ✉ 11 Polson Street
☎ 416/461-DOCK 🚇 Union

BARS

BAR ITALIA

The slick spot in Little Italy for the young and the beautiful. Upstairs there's a plush pool area. Downstairs it's coffee, alcoholic drinks, and Italian specialties all round.

✚ G7 ✉ 582 College Street ☎ 416/535-3621 🚋 College Street streetcar

C'EST WHAT

A cellar-style bar that's very casual and comfortable. You can relax and enjoy quiet conversation while you listen to whatever folk-acoustic group is playing.

✚ K9 ✉ 67 Front Street East ☎ 416/867-9499 🚇 Union

FIONN MACCOOL'S

In the heart of downtown, Fionn MacCool's features English and Irish beers on tap, and traditional foods like pies, pasties, coddles, and fish and chips. Live Celtic music most nights attracts a Toronto microcosm of students, business people, and those looking for a taste of home.

✚ K9 ✉ 35 The Esplanade (corner of Church and The Esplanade) ☎ 416/362-2495 🚇 Union

LA SERRE

The Four Seasons hotel bar. Singled out as one of the best bars in the city by *Forbes Magazine*, it offers great martinis, a full range of single malt whiskies and other specialty items.

✚ J6 ✉ Four Seasons Hotel 21 Avenue Road ☎ 416/964-0411 🚇 Bay

ORBIT ROOM

This agreeable little bar is a haunt of local professional people, who like to gather upstairs. Comfortable, old-fashioned atmosphere, with semicircular banquettes and etched glass. Entertainment provided by local groups.

✚ G7 ✉ 580A College Street ☎ 416/535-0613 🚋 College Street streetcar

ROTTERDAM

This is the place for serious beer drinkers—Bavarian-style beers and ales are brewed in huge tanks. About ten brews are on tap. It gets crowded later in the evening. Good summer patio.

✚ H8 ✉ 600 King Street West (at Portland) ☎ 416/504-6882 🚋 King Street streetcar

SOUZ DAL

A small hideaway with a Moroccan atmosphere including a copper bar and kilim wall hangings. The inviting candelit patio under a trellis is a romantic spot to indulge in fruit-flavored martinis on summer evenings.

✚ G7 ✉ 636 College Street ☎ 416/537-1883 🚋 College Street streetcar

WAYNE GRETZKY'S

A shrine to the Canadian hockey player. Forget the food and head upstairs to the rooftop outdoor patio, which has great views out over the gardenias. Memorabilia decorate the long bar downstairs.

✚ H9 ✉ 99 Blue Jays Way ☎ 416/979-7825 🚇 St. Andrew

Gay Toronto

To get a fix on the scene, pick up *Xtra!* or go to Gay Liberation Bookstore/Glad Day Bookshop (✚ K6 ✉ 598a Yonge Street ☎ 416/961-4161).

Among the long-standing popular bars are Woody's (✚ K7 ✉ 467 Church Street ☎ 416/972-0887); The Barn/The Stables (✚ K7 ✉ 418 Church Street ☎ 416/977-4702); Pints (✚ K7 ✉ 518 Church Street ☎ 416/921-8142), where the patio is jammed in summer; and Tallulah's Cabaret (✚ K7 ✉ 12 Alexander Street ☎ 416/975-8555) is the place to flaunt yourself and your dance technique to alternative music. Friday is supposedly women's night.

LUXURY HOTELS

Hotel prices

Expect to pay the following prices per night for a double room, but it's always worth asking when you make your reservation whether any special deals are available.

Budget   up to $60
Mid-range   up to $110
Luxury   more than $175

Country luxury

For a languorous country-house experience convenient for Stratford (➤ 20), book a room at Langdon Hall. Built in 1902, it stands in 200 acres and offers superb accommodation set around a cloister garden. The main house has a lovely dining room and conservatory. Facilities include outdoor pool, tennis court, croquet lawn, billiards room, spa-fitness center, and cross-country ski trails.

✉ RR 3, Cambridge, ON N3H 4R8 ☎ 519/740-2100

FOUR SEASONS

In the center of Yorkville, this is the city's top hotel. The service is personal yet unobtrusive, the 380 rooms spacious, elegant, comfortable and well equipped, and the facilities excellent. It has a world-class restaurant, Truffles (➤ 63), a great bar, La Serre (➤ 83), and the Studio Café attracts a celebrity crowd.

✛ J6 ✉ 21 Avenue Road ☎ 416/964-0411; fax 964-2301 ⊙ Bay

INTERCONTINENTAL

With 209 rooms, this stylish hotel around the corner from Yorkville provides a large measure of personal service. Spacious rooms with elegant Louis XVI-style furnishings offer every comfort. The Signatures bar, with its cherry paneling and fireplace, is a favorite rendezvous for afternoon tea or cocktails.

✛ J6 ✉ 220 Bloor Street West ☎ 416/960-5200; fax 960-8269 ⊙ St. George

METROPOLITAN

A challenger to the Four Seasons in terms of its restaurants, which are spectacularly decorated; service is less splendid.

✛ J8 ✉ 108 Chestnut Street ☎ 416/977-5000; fax 977-9513 ⊙ St. Patrick

PARK HYATT

A stylish classic. The 64 rooms and two suites in the original towers have been recently renovated to an exceptional standard with fine fabrics and furnishings and the latest in amenities.

There are four restaurants.

✛ J6 ✉ 4 Avenue Road ☎ 416/924-5471 or 800/977 4197; fax 924-6693 ⊙ Bay, Museum

ROYAL MERIDIEN KING EDWARD

The city's most venerable hotel, which has welcomed such guests as Edward, Prince of Wales, and Rudolph Valentino. An architectural jewel, featuring marble and sculpted stucco. The Victoria Room is a favorite gathering place. The 299 rooms are very spacious, handsomely decorated, and well equipped.

✛ K8 ✉ 37 King Street East ☎ 416/863-9700; fax 367-5515 ⊙ King

SUTTON PLACE

This hotel has seen some ups and downs over the years, but is back on form. Restaurant and bar, fitness facilities, indoor pool and sundeck, and a business center. 260 rooms.

✛ J6-J7 ✉ 955 Bay Street ☎ 416/924-9221 or 800/268-3790; fax 924-1778 ⊙ Museum, Wellesley

WESTIN HARBOUR CASTLE

Although large and hosting many conventions, this hotel's lakefront location and facilities put it in the luxury category. Many of the 980 rooms have a view of the lake. Includes a revolving and a Chinese restaurant (Grand Yatt). Squash courts, tennis court and indoor pool.

✛ K9 ✉ 1 Harbour Square ☎ 416/869-1600 or 800/228-3000; fax 869-0573 ⊙ Union

MID-RANGE HOTELS

DELTA CHELSEA
Large and well-run, with excellent facilities for children (a supervised creative center for 3-to 8-year-olds). Two pools.
🕂 J7 ✉ 33 Gerrard Street West ☎ 416/595-1975 or 800/243-5732; fax 585-4375 🚇 College

HILTON INTERNATIONAL
Typical Hilton near the convention center and financial district. Indoor/outdoor pool.
🕂 J8 ✉ 145 Richmond Street West ☎ 416/869-3456 or 800/445-8667; fax 869-3187 🚇 Osgoode

MARRIOTT
Very conveniently close to the Eaton Centre, this hotel has well-equipped rooms and a rooftop pool.
🕂 J8 ✉ 525 Bay Street ☎ 416/597-9200; fax 597-9211 🚇 Dundas

RADISSON PLAZA HOTEL ADMIRAL
Harbourfront hotel with rooftop pool, bar, and terrace. The 157 rooms are well furnished and equipped. Squash court, two restaurants, and a bar.
🕂 J9 ✉ 249 Queen's Quay West ☎ 416/203-3333 or 800/333-3333; fax 203-3100 🚇 Union then LRT

ROYAL YORK
Rooms vary in style and size and the service can be overtaxed as there are 1,365 rooms. Ten bars and restaurants—the Library Bar is noted for martinis, and the Acadian Room for its Canadian cuisine. Pool.
🕂 J9 ✉ 100 Front Street West

☎ 416/368-2511 or 863 6333 (reservations only); fax 368-2884 🚇 Union

SHERATON
Although the city's largest hotel (1,377 rooms), the Sheraton offers efficient service. Six restaurants and bars and a theater.
🕂 J8 ✉ 123 Queen Street West ☎ 416/361-1000; fax 947-4874 🚇 Osgoode

SKYDOME
Out of 346 rooms, 70 overlook the baseball turf at SkyDome. Rooms are functional and modern. Swimming pool, fitness center and squash courts.
🕂 H9 ✉ 1 Blue Jays Way ☎ 416/341-7100; fax 341-5090 🚇 Union

WESTIN PRINCE
Set in 15 acres, this Japanese-owned hotel is 20 minutes from downtown in the Don Valley. The rooms are serenely decorated. Katsura restaurant offers sushi and *robata* bars, tempura counter, and teppanyaki-style cuisine (the chef grills in front of you). Putting green, tennis courts, fitness center.
🕂 Off map to northeast ✉ 900 York Mills Road, Don Mills ☎ 416/444-2511; fax 444-9597 🚇 York Mills

WYNDHAM BRISTOL PLACE
The best hotel on the airport strip. Rooms are well furnished and fully equipped. Indoor/outdoor pool and fitness facility.
🕂 Off map to northwest ✉ 950 Dixon Road ☎ 416/675-9444; fax 675-4426 🚇 Kipling

Bed & breakfast
Several bed and breakfast organizations help visitors to find rooms in private homes from $50 to $100 a night.

Toronto Bed & Breakfast
✉ Box 269, 253 College Street, ON M5T 1R5 ☎ 416/588-8800

Downtown Toronto Association of Bed and Breakfast Guesthouses
✉ Box 190, Station B, ON M5T 2W1 ☎ 416/368-1420

BUDGET HOTELS

Dorms and hostels

In summer, university dorms provide fine budget accommodations. Neil Wycik (✚ K7 ✉ 96 Gerrard Street East ☎ 416/977-2320; fax 977-2809) and Victoria University (✚ J6 ✉ 140 Charles Street West ☎ 416/585-4524; fax 585-4530) are both conveniently located downtown. Other accommodation can be found at University of Toronto in Scarborough (☎ 416/287-7369; fax 287-7667). There are comfortable rooms and excellent facilities (TV lounge, kitchen, laundry, indoor pool, tennis courts, and fitness center) at the downtown hostel (✚ K8 ✉ 76 Church Street at King ☎ 416/971-4440; fax 971-4088).

BOND PLACE

An established, medium-sized hotel. Restaurant and lounge.
✚ K8 ✉ 65 Dundas Street East ☎ 416/362-6061; fax 360-6406 🚇 Dundas

COMFORT INN

Only two blocks south of Bloor, this 113-room hotel has large rooms and a restaurant on the premises. Guests have access to nearby health club for a small fee.
✚ K6 ✉ 15 Charles Street East ☎ 416/924-1222; fax 927-1369 🚇 Bloor-Yonge

DAYS INN

Right next door to Maple Leaf Gardens, this modern high-rise hotel has reason-ably priced rooms, sports bar, restaurant, and an indoor pool.
✚ K7 ✉ 30 Carlton Street ☎ 416/977-6655; fax 977-0502 🚇 College

HOLIDAY INN ON KING

Modern well-equipped rooms at a very good price for the location (across from the Convention Centre). Downstairs restaurant-bar.
✚ H8 ✉ 370 King Street West at Peter ☎ 416/599-4000; fax 599-7394 🚇 St. Andrew

HOTEL SELBY

Located in a handsome Victorian building, this midtown hotel is good value. High-ceilinged rooms are individually decorated and furnished. Coin laundry on site. Guests have access to health club nearby for a small fee. Relaxed, gay-friendly atmosphere.
✚ K6 ✉ 592 Sherbourne ☎ 416/921-3142; fax 923-3177 🚇 Sherbourne

HOTEL VICTORIA

In the Financial District with only 54 small rooms. Some have coffeemakers and mini-refrigerators. Restaurant and lounge.
✚ K9 ✉ 56 Yonge Street ☎ 416/363-1666; fax 363-7327 🚇 King

QUALITY HOTEL

Not far from the heart of the financial district, this 196-room hotel has modern rooms. No dining or other special facilities.
✚ K8 ✉ 111 Lombard Street between Adelaide and Richmond ☎ 416/367-5555; fax 367-3470 🚇 King, Queen

STRATHCONA

Decent, if small, rooms at a fraction of the price of the Royal York right opposite. Coffee shop-restaurant, sports bar, and room service 6AM–7PM.
✚ J9 ✉ 60 York Street ☎ 416/363-3321; fax 363-4679 🚇 Union

VENTURE INN, YORKVILLE

Great Yorkville location and good value with very reasonably priced modern rooms (there are only 70, so make a reservation). No additional facilities.
✚ J5 ✉ 89 Avenue Road ☎ 416/964-1220; fax 964-8692 🚇 Bay, St. George

TORONTO
travel facts

ARRIVING & DEPARTING

Before you go

- U.S. citizens and legal residents do not need passports, but must show proof of citizenship (birth or voter's certificate, naturalization papers, or green card).
- Citizens of other countries must have passports and many will also need visas. Allow plenty of time to apply for a visa at a local Canadian embassy or consulate.
- Every person under 18 must have a letter from a parent or guardian granting them permission to travel to Canada. It should state the name of the traveler and the duration of the trip.

When to go

- Toronto's winters can be harsh, with freezing temperatures that are made worse by the unrelenting winds blowing off Lake Ontario.
- Spring is unpredictable. Occasional snow or ice storms can occur as late as mid-April, but the winter has usually vanished by the end of April.
- Summer is the best time to visit Toronto, when Ontario Place and Canada's Wonderland and all the other attractions open, and the ferries to the islands are in full swing.
- Autumn is also a good time to visit. The weather is still warm, and outside the city the forests take on a rich golden glow.

Climate

- Average temperatures:
  Jan 18° to 34°F; Feb 20° to 30°F; Mar 28° to 37°F; Apr 37° to 54°F; May 48° to 62°F; Jun 55° to 74°F; Jul 61° to 79°F; Aug 59° to 77°F; Sep 54° to 72°F; Oct 44° to 57°F; Nov 36° to 45°F; Dec 21° to 36°F

Arriving by air

- Pearson International Airport lies northwest of the city about 18 miles or 30–60 minutes from downtown.
- There are three terminals at the airport. Most international flights arrive at Trillium Terminal 3.
- A taxi (special airport taxis) costs $40–$45, plus tip, to downtown.
- Bus: Airport Express Bus ☎ 905/564-6333 or 564-3232 serves six downtown hotels and major terminals, leaving every 20 minutes.
- The airport is served by bus and subway to Islington, York Mills or Yorkdale stations—these save around $4–$5 over the Airport Express.

Arriving by bus

- Long-distance and commuter buses arrive at the Metro Coach Terminal at 610 Bay Street near Dundas.

Arriving by car

- The U.S. highway system leads directly into Canada. If you are driving from Michigan, you will enter at Detroit-Windsor (via I-75 and the Ambassador Bridge) or Port Huron-Sarnia (via I-94 and the Bluewater Bridge). From New York State, using I-90 you can enter at Buffalo-Fort Erie; Niagara Falls, NY-Niagara Falls, Ont; or Niagara Falls, NY-Lewiston. Using I-81, you can cross at Hill Island; using route 37, you will cross either at Ogdensburg-Johnstown or Rooseveltown-Cornwall. Once across the border, you approach Toronto from the west by the Queen Elizabeth Way or Highway 401, from the east by Highway 2 or Highway 401.
- Approximate distances to Toronto are: Boston 565 miles; Buffalo 95

miles; Chicago 530 miles; New York 495 miles.
- You will need to carry your driver's license, car registration, and proof of auto insurance.

Arriving by train
- Commuter (GO trains) and long-distance trains (VIA Rail in Canada, Amtrak in the U.S.) arrive at Union Station which is linked directly to the subway.

Customs regulations
- U.S. visitors over 18 may bring in free of duty up to 50 cigars, 200 cigarettes and 1kg of tobacco; 1.14 liters of liquor or wine may be imported by travelers over the minimum drinking age of the province to be visited (19 in Ontario). You may bring in gifts up to Can$60.
- No firearms, plants, or meats may be imported.
- Information from Revenue Canada ✉ 875 Heron Road, Ottawa, ON KIA OL8 ☎ 416/973-8022

ESSENTIAL FACTS

Insurance
- Make sure you have a policy covering accident, medical expenses, personal liability, trip cancellation and interruption, delayed departure, and loss or theft of personal property.
- If you plan to rent a car, check to make sure that you are covered for collision, personal accident, liability, and theft or loss. Most credit card companies provide primary or secondary collision/damage insurance and your home insurance policy may cover loss and theft, but liability is rarely covered for overseas travel.

Money matters
- Most banks have automated teller machines (ATMs) that are linked to Cirrus, Plus, or other networks and this is the easiest way to secure cash. However, before you leave check that your PIN number is valid in Canada. Also check on frequency and amount limits. For locations contact Cirrus from anywhere in the world ☎ 800/424-7787 or Plus (only in the U.S.) ☎ 800/843-7587
- Credit cards are widely accepted. American Express, Diner's Club, Discover, MasterCard, and Visa are the most common.
- Traveler's checks are accepted in all but small stores as long as the denominations are small ($20 or $50). If you carry traveler's checks in Canadian dollars, you save on conversion fees.

National holidays
- January 1
Good Friday and/or
Easter Monday
Victoria Day (third Monday in May)
Canada Day (July 1)
Civic Holiday (first Monday in August)
Labour Day (first Monday in September)
Thanksgiving (second Monday in October)
Remembrance Day (Nov 11)
Christmas Day (Dec 25) and
Boxing Day (Dec 26)

Opening hours
- Banks: generally Mon–Thu 10–3; Fri 10–6.
- Museums: hours vary.
- Post Office: generally Mon–Fri 8–5:30. Stamps and minimal post office services are available at drugstores and general stores and they are often open outside post office hours.

- Shops: generally Mon–Wed 9:30 or 10–6; Sat, Sun 10–5. Hours are also often extended on Thu or Fri until 8 or 9.

Places of worship

- Baptist: Rosedale Baptist Church ✉ 877 Yonge Street ☎ 416/926-0732
- Episcopal: St. James' Cathedral ✉ 65 Church Street, at King ☎ 416/364-7865
- Jewish: Beth Shalom Synagogue (Conservative), Holy Blossom Temple (Refroem) ✉ 1445 Eglinton Avenue West ☎ 416/783-6103
- Presbyterian: St. Andrew's ✉ 75 Simcoe Sreet ☎ 416/593-5600
- Roman Catholic: St. Michael's Cathedral ✉ 200 Church Street ☎ 416/364-0234

Safety

- Toronto is considerably safer than most North American cities, but there is always danger of theft, and visitors need to exercise some caution in crowded areas and on the subway. Use common sense.
- Some areas should be avoided. Downtown, avoid Moss Park, and don't enter Allan Gardens and High Park at night.

Smoking

- In 1993 smoking was banned in all public buildings, except in clearly designated smoking areas. By 2001 all bars and restaurants are expected to be no smoking.

Student travelers

- An International Student Identity Card (ISIC) reduces admission at some museums, theaters, and other attractions.
- Always carry a photo ID to prove your age. That way you won't be excluded from bars and clubs unless you are under age.
- Under-25s will find it hard to rent a car.

Taxes

- The provincial retail sales tax is 8 percent; there is also a 5 percent tax on hotel/motel rooms, and a national goods and services tax (GST) of 7 percent.
- Nonresidents can apply for a refund of taxes on non-disposable merchandise that is taken out of the country within 60 days of purchase (► 71). Meals and restaurant charges, car rentals, hotel accommodations, and similar services do not qualify for the rebate.
- Information from Visitor Rebate Programme ✉ Revenue Canada, Summerside Tax Centre, Summerside PE C1N 6C6 ☎ 902/432-5608

Time differences

- Toronto is on Eastern Standard Time, the same as New York City. Daylight saving time, when clocks are moved one hour forward, is in effect from April through October.

Tipping

- As a rule, tip around 15 percent in restaurants and bars, 15–20 percent to cab drivers, $1 per bag to porters, and $1 to a valet parking attendant. Hairdressers also expect 15–20 percent.

Restrooms

- Municipal restrooms are rare. Use the restrooms in major shopping complexes and hotel lobbies, bars, and restaurants.

Visitors with disabilities

- Much of the city has been built in the last 20 years and many buildings are barrier free and well equipped with elevators for easy wheelchair access.
- The subway is not accessible, but the city operates a special transport service, Wheel-Trans, for

which visitors can register. For information ☎ 416/393-4111

- Parking privileges are extended to drivers who have disabled plates or a special pass allowing parking in "No Parking" zones.
- For more detailed information, Disabled Information on Community Services ✉ Community Information Centre of Metropolitan Toronto, 425 Adelaide Street West, Toronto, ON M5V 3C1 ☎ 416/392-0505 🕐 Daily 8AM–10PM

Women travelers

- Women will find Toronto hospitable and relatively safe (but see Safety opposite).
- For books and information stop by the Toronto Women's Bookstore ✉ 73 Harbord Street at Spadina ☎ 416/922-8744 🕐 Daily from 10:30 on weekdays, from noon Sun

PUBLIC TRANSPORTATION

Subway and buses

- The subway is fast, quiet, clean, and easy to use. It consists of two lines—Bloor–Danforth and Yonge–University–Spadina. The first runs east–west from Kipling Avenue in the west to Kennedy Road in the east, where it connects with Scarborough Rapid Transit. The second runs from Finch Avenue in the north to Union Station, where it loops north along University Avenue connecting with the Bloor Line at St. George before proceeding to Wilson Avenue.
- You need a tiny token costing $2 to ride the subway ($1.35 for students 19 and under and senior citizens, 50c for children under 12). Drop it into the box at the ticket window or into the turnstile. To save money, purchase ten tokens for $16 ($10.70 for

students and senior citizens, $4 for children). Day, monthly, and annual passes are also available.

- The subway system is connected to the bus and streetcar network. It is always wise to pick up a transfer at the subway station from the push-button machine at the entrance or from the bus driver. By so doing, you can board a streetcar going east or west from the subway station if you need to, or transfer from the bus to the subway without paying extra.
- The subway operates Mon–Fri 6AM–1:30AM and Sun 9AM–1:30AM. A Blue Night Network is in operation outside those hours on basic surface routes, running about every 30 minutes.
- To ride the buses and streetcars you need a transfer, a token, or exact change. Bus stops are located at or near corners and are marked by elongated signs with red stripes and diagrams of a bus and streetcar (but be warned—they are not always easy to see). Bus routes are shown on the Ride Guide map, which is an essential accessory.
- From Union Station a Light Rapid Transit (LRT) line operates to Harbourfront, stopping between Queen's Quay and Rees Street. NB No transfer is needed to ride the LRT.
- For transit information pick up a Ride Guide at a subway station or call ☎ 416/393-4636 (7AM–10PM)

Taxis

- Cabs can be hailed on the street. The light on the rooftop will be turned on if the taxi is available.

- All taxis must display rates and contain a meter. Receipts are available.
- Tip 15–20 percent.

DRIVING

- U.S. visitors should note the following local laws: city speed limit is 30 miles; right turns are permitted unless posted otherwise; seat belts are compulsory; parking penalties include being towed. It is advisable to obtain an International Driving Permit to hire a car.

MEDIA & COMMUNICATIONS

Telephones

- Public payphones can be found everywhere—and there is often even a telephone directory available.
- To dial outside the area codes of 416 or 905 add the prefix 1.
- To avoid hefty hotel surcharges on local calls use payphones. For long distance use AT&T, MCI or Sprint rather than calling direct. Access codes and instructions are found on your phone card. If they don't work, dial the operator and ask for the access code in Canada.

Post offices

- The Post Office in Canada has been withdrawing from direct customer service. Postal services can be found at convenience and drugstores like Shopper's Drug Mart. Look for a sign in the window advertising postal services.
- There are also post office windows open in major shopping complexes like Atrium on the Bay ✚ J7–J8 ☎ 416/506-0911 Commerce Court ✚ J8–J9 ☎ 416/956-7452

Toronto Dominion Centre ✚ J8–J9 ☎ 416/360-7105 and First Canadian Place ✚ J8 ☎ 416/364-0540

Newspapers

- There are four local dailies: the *Globe & Mail*, which is the heavyweight, and the *Toronto Star* and *Toronto Sun*. The *National Post* was launched in 1998 to challenge the *Globe*. There are also free papers like *Eye* and *Now*, essential for arts/entertainment listings, and *Xtra!* for its gay listings. There are also ethnic newspapers serving local communities.

Magazines

- *Toronto Life* is the major monthly city magazine. *Where Toronto* is usually provided free in your hotel room.

International newsagents

- There are several chains that sell international newspapers and magazines. The main ones are Great Canadian News and Lichtman's, with several outlets in town, and the Maison de la Presse Internationale ✉ 124 Yorkville Avenue ☎ 416/928-2328

Radio

- CBC Radio offers assorted programming from serious talk and drama to classical and other music as well as news. It broadcasts on 94.1 FM and 740 AM.
- Broadcasting in 30 languages, CHIN at 100.7 FM and 1540 AM puts visitors in touch with the ethnic/multicultural scene.

Television

- Hotels usually receive all the channels available to cable subscribers. This includes CBC along with the major American networks like PBS, plus CNN and other cable stations such as Much Music, Toronto's version of MTV produced by Citytv.

EMERGENCIES

Emergency phone numbers

- Fire, police and ambulance ☎ 911
- Metro police station ✉ 40 College Street ☎ 416/808-2222
- Rape Crisis ☎ 416/597-8808
- Victim Assault ☎ 416/863-0511

Embassies and Consulates

- All embassies are in the national capital Ottawa.
- The following consulates are found in Toronto:
- U.S.A. ✉ 360 University Avenue ☎ 416/595-1700
- Australia ✉ 175 Bloor Street East ☎ 416/323-1155
- U.K. ✉ 777 Bay Street at College ☎ 416/593-1267

Lost property

- For articles left on a bus, streetcar or subway, TTC Lost Articles Office ✉ Bay Street subway station ☎ 416/393-4100 ⊙ Mon–Fri 8–5
- If you lose a credit card or traveler's checks, report the loss immediately to the credit card company or the company issuing the checks, and to the local police. Main international credit card phone numbers: American Express ☎ 336/393-1111 (call collect) Diner's Club ☎ 1/800/ 234-6377 MasterCard ☎ 1/800/ 826-2181 Visa ☎ 1/800/336-8472

Medical and dental treatment

- 24-hour emergency service is provided by the Toronto General Hospital ☎ 416/340-3111. The main entrance is at 200 Elizabeth Street, another entrance is at 150 Gerrard Street West.

- If you need a doctor, inquire at your hotel or seek a referral from the College of Physicians and Surgeons ✉ 80 College Street ☎ 416/961-1711 ⊙ 9–5
- In the event of a dental emergency ask for a referral from the Ontario Dental Association ☎ 416/922-3900

Medicines

- Always bring a prescription for any medications in case of loss and also to show to the customs officers if necessary.
- Shopper's Drug Mart ✉ 360 Bloor Street West stays open daily until midnight. Several downtown locations are open 24 hours. Pharma Plus ✉ 68 Wellesley Street at Church ☎ 416/924-7760 is also open until midnight.

VISITOR INFORMATION

- You can obtain information from: Tourism Toronto ✉ 207 Queen's Quay West, suite 590, in the Queen's Quay Terminal ☎ 416/203-2500 or 800/363-1990 ⊙ Summer: Mon–Thu 8:30–8; Fri 8:30–5; Sat 9–5; Sun 9:30–5. Winter: Mon–Fri 8:30–5 The visitor information center in Eaton Centre is open daily.
- For Ontario provincial information contact Ontario Travel ✉ Queen's Park, ON M7A 2R9 ☎ 416/314-0944 or 800/ONTARIO

Index

Citypack
Toronto

Time inevitably brings change, so always confirm prices, travel facts, and other perishable information when it matters. Although Fodor's cannot accept responsibility for errors, you can use this guide in the confidence that we have taken every care to ensure its accuracy.

ISBN 0-679-00485-8
Second Edition

FODOR'S CITYPACK TORONTO

AUTHOR *Marilyn Wood*
CARTOGRAPHY *The Automobile Association*
RV Reiser-und Verkehrsverlag GmbH
COVER DESIGN *Fabrizio La Rocca, Tigist Getachew*
VERIFIER *Sara Waxman*
SECOND EDITION UPDATED BY *Marilyn Wood*

Acknowledgements

The Automobile Association wishes to thank the following photographers, libraries and associations for their assistance in the preparation of this book: Black Creek Pioneer Village 27a (K. Bray), 27b; Comstock 31a (Malak), 31b (K. Sommerer), 43a (E. Otto), 43b (F. Grant), 46 (E. Otto), 56 (E. Otto); Harbourfront Antique Market, Toronto, 34a, 34b; Larter Associates Inc. 45b Centreville; McMichael Canadian Art Collection 25, a detail from *The Red Maple 1914* by A. Y. Jackson 1882-1974, gift of Mr S. Walter Stewart; Toronto Metro Zoo 48; Ontario Science Centre 47a; Paramount Canada's Wonderland 23b, 26a, 26b; Pictures Colour Library 18, 28a; Royal Botanical Gardens, Ontario 24; Spectrum Colour Library 42a; Zefa Pictures Ltd. 19a, 28b, 45a, 50b, 52, 54b, 59, 60. All remaining photographs were taken by Jon Davison and are held in the Association's own library (AA Photo Library) with the exception of the following pages: Jeff Beazley 30a, 49b, 50a, 53b, 54a, 61a and Jean-François Pin 5a, 5b, 6/7, 8, 12, 13a, 20, 21a, 35a, 37, 49a, 55, 57.

Color separation by Daylight Colour Art Pte Ltd, Singapore
Manufactured by Dai Nippon Printing Co. (Hong Kong) Ltd.
10 9 8 7 6 5 4 3 2 1

Titles in the Citypack series

- Amsterdam • Atlanta • Beijing • Berlin • Boston • Chicago • Dublin •
- Florence • Hong Kong • London • Los Angeles • Miami • Montreal •
- New York • Paris • Prague • Rome • San Francisco • Seattle • Shanghai •
- Sydney • Tokyo • Toronto • Venice • Washington, D.C. •